Grasshopper Pueblo

Grasshopper Pueblo

A Story of Archaeology and Ancient Life

Jefferson Reid and Stephanie Whittlesey

The University of Arizona Press » Tucson

First printing
The University of Arizona Press
© 1999 The Arizona Board of Regents
All rights reserved
⊜ This book is printed on acid-free, archival-quality paper.
Manufactured in the United States of America
04   03   02   01   00   99   6   5   4   3   2   1

Library of Congress Cataloging-in-Publication Data
Reid, J. Jefferson.
    Grasshopper Pueblo : a story of archaeology and ancient life / Jefferson Reid
and Stephanie Whittlesey.
        p.   cm.
    Includes bibliographical references and index.
    ISBN 0-8165-1913-7 (cloth : alk. paper)
    ISBN 0-8165-1914-5 (pbk. : alk. paper)
    1. Grasshopper Pueblo (Ariz.)   2. Mogollon culture.   3. Archaeology—
Methodology.   I. Whittlesey, Stephanie Michelle.   II. Title.
    E99.M76   R45   1999
    979.1′59—dc21   99-6572
                                                              CIP

British Library Cataloguing-in-Publication Data
A catalogue record for this book is available from the British Library.

Publication of this book is made possible in part by a grant from the Provost's
Author Support Fund of the University of Arizona.

Contents

Figures

Preface

Our story—a popular ethnography of the life and times of a fourteenth-century pueblo community in the mountains of east-central Arizona, called Grasshopper Pueblo—is not just a documentary of a particular moment in the past. Nor is it an exposé of ancient mysteries or an account of how romantic and adventuresome the life of an archaeologist can be, although such stories can make fascinating reading. The everyday life of the ancient people, named the Mogollon by archaeologists, who lived at Grasshopper Pueblo was more or less uncomplicated. The simple joys and small rewards of this life and the typical problems that these people faced are readily recognizable to contemporary readers. Embedded in our account are modest truths that tell us much about our unique human capacities. Our story, in addition to painting a picture of the past, reveals what we hope are significant features of human culture, human spirit, and the ultimate value of archaeology to contemporary society.

It is also a unique story, one that will not be matched in our lifetimes, if perhaps ever. Although large pueblos of the American Southwest have attracted archaeologists for more than a century, few have been excavated with any degree of thoroughness, and fewer still have ever been interpreted in terms that the general reader can comprehend easily. Ancient life at these special places will never be understood with as much detail as we have for Grasshopper Pueblo, even though some of these pueblos—Point of Pines, Awat'ovi, Bailey Ruin, Hawikuh, Chavez Pass Ruin—have witnessed archaeological study, and others—Homol'ovi, Kinishba, Cliff Palace, and Pueblo Bonito—have been the focus of public outreach and interpretation. Sadly, many others are gone, fallen prey to modern development and vandalism.

There are three prominent reasons for the uniqueness of the Grasshopper research, independent of our deep attachment to the place and its past. First is that 105 rooms, representing a little more than 20 percent of the pueblo, were excavated, and they provide an unusually large sample of rooms and artifacts. Second is the quantity and quality of the artifact record itself. Grasshopper, like similar mountain pueblo ruins, is remarkable in having whole pots and nonperishable tools left on room floors, as though the inhabitants left behind their household belongings in anticipation of a return that never happened. There is no evidence for a catastrophe that would have forced a sudden departure. In addition, the fill of a single Grasshopper room may easily contain more broken pieces of pottery than entire sites in other regions of the Southwest.

The third reason for Grasshopper's uniqueness derives from the growing concern by Native Americans for actively participating in the interpretation of their history and taking control of managing cultural resources on their lands. As one example of this important trend, we offer changing attitudes toward the excavation of human remains. Grasshopper research began in 1963, at a time when it was standard scientific practice to excavate human burials. Cemetery areas were sought and excavated to develop a reliable sample of biological data and mortuary artifacts.

By 1979, when Reid took over as director of Grasshopper research, approximately seven hundred of the inhabitants of Grasshopper Pueblo had been found and studied by archaeologists. Discussions that year between Reid and Ronnie Lupe, then chairman of the White Mountain Apache Tribe on whose land Grasshopper Pueblo is located, resulted in a decision to cease further excavation of human remains at Grasshopper, in accord with Apache values and wishes. This took place eleven years prior to the passage of the federal Native American Graves Protection and Repatriation Act, which ef-

Jefferson Reid discusses Grasshopper archaeology with representatives of the White Mountain Apache tribal management and enforcement agencies.

fectively halted the traditional archaeological practice of burial excavation in the United States.

Before the seven hundred inhabitants of Grasshopper are returned to the earth, they will have given us a comprehensive picture of the biological conditions of pueblo life and valuable insights into ceremonial life and the organization of Grasshopper Pueblo through the artifacts of their mortuary ritual. Archaeologists and biological anthropologists may never again be able to report on the physical condition and health of an entire community and not just an isolated individual. The special character of Grasshopper Pueblo and the people who lived there will become apparent as their story unfolds in the following pages.

We have two important goals in offering this book. The first is to summarize what we know, what we think we know, and what we suspect about life at Grasshopper Pueblo, so that this information can be used as a guide for the next generation of Grasshopper researchers. Our combined research experience of almost sixty years' duration joins with our conjectures, intuitions, and the research of many others to form the archaeological synthesis that is the story of Grasshopper. There are no others who can answer the many questions that students and researchers are likely to have in the future. This book, we hope, will serve that research need.

Second, we aspire to craft a story for the benefit of the nonarchaeologist— for the Western Apache and other Native American peoples and for the vast audience of non-Indians wishing to understand southwestern prehistory. We seek to present a story that will explain our myriad reasons for spending twenty years in the sun and dirt on a remote Indian reservation seemingly at the ends of the earth. We would be gratified if other Native Americans as well as the Western Apache find the Grasshopper story interesting and useful.

Additionally, we hope this book and the story it contains will appeal to interested nonprofessionals who find the American Southwest a vital and fascinating place and its peoples past and present worth knowing. We would also be happy if our archaeological colleagues seek out this book. Although we have tried to eliminate the jargon and the technical baggage that can make archaeological treatises almost incomprehensible, we have not sensationalized the Grasshopper story for the benefit of the reader. It is as close to truth as any archaeology ever comes. The educational goal of this book, therefore, is to reach all those people interested in a thorough account of Indian life in the prehistoric past. To enhance the educational goal of this book, we assign all profits from its sale to benefit the Cibecue Apache.

The Apache say, so anthropologist Keith Basso tells us, that "the land is always stalking people. The land makes people live right. The land looks after us." The places have names, and the names are like pictures that tell stories. "Stories," the Apache say, "go to work on you like arrows. Stories make you live right. Stories make you replace yourself." Grasshopper Pueblo is one such place. It has a name, and its name tells stories—stories of renewal and hope, of abandonment and beginning anew, of past lives and future dreams. It has been six years since we left, and Grasshopper still works on us like arrows.

Acknowledgments

The idea for this book began more than twenty years ago with the award to the senior author of a National Science Foundation Grant (BNS 74-23724 AO1) entitled "Grasshopper, a Late Mogollon Community in East-Central Arizona: A Proposed Monograph." Most of the parts of that monograph have appeared over the past decades as the many products of research by us and the scores of students who have gone through the University of Arizona Archaeological Field School at Grasshopper. All that remained was this book-length synthesis. This summary of ancient life at Grasshopper Pueblo could not have been written without the blood, sweat, and tears of thirty years of field school students and staff. Among these unnamed legions, we are indebted most to those whose research we have used and to reviewers of the book manuscript: Joseph Ezzo, Julie Lowell, Barbara Montgomery, Charles Riggs, Raymond Thompson, John Welch and two anonymous reviewers.

Joseph Wilder, director of the Southwest Center, and the Faculty Fellows program, both of the University of Arizona, provided funds for Charles Riggs's drawings and for the photographic assistance of Kathy Hubenschmidt, Susan Luebbermann, and Ken Matesich of the Arizona State Museum. Funds to make this book affordable to a general audience came from the Grasshopper publication fund, the Provost's Author Support Fund, and Michael Cusanovich, vice president for research, all of the University of Arizona.

These acknowledgments cannot express fully our heartfelt thanks to the White Mountain Apache, who encouraged, assisted, and worked alongside the archaeologists for nearly thirty years. These include a long line of tribal chairmen, especially Ronnie Lupe; tribal council members, particularly the late Nashley Tessay Sr.; and the people of Cibecue, most notably the Glenn Cromwell family, the many families of Tessays, and the many Quays. Because we owe them much but cannot name them all, this book is dedicated to the Cibecue Apache.

Grasshopper Pueblo

1

The Land, the People, and the Place

Grasshopper is a place with many pasts where people of different cultures came together, lived for a time, then left to begin anew elsewhere. As a speck on the map of Arizona, it is not much different from hundreds of other places on the sweeping landscape of the American Southwest. Yet that dot on the map labels a unique place, one that takes its special character from the people who lived there for a short time, from the landscape in which they strived, and from the rich catalog of material artifacts they left behind for archaeologists to decipher.

Grasshopper lies in the heart of the rugged mountain country of central Arizona on the Fort Apache Reservation some 14 miles west of the Apache village of Cibecue—Deeschii' Bikoh, "red canyon, standing horizontally," or "valley with long red bluffs," in the Western Apache language. Once the road to Grasshopper was impassable when winter snow and summer thunderstorms turned it to

Daniela Triadan, field school staff member and excavation supervisor, uses a transit to map artifacts.

thick red mud. Today it is graded and graveled, built for enormous logging trucks. Just past the Cibecue school, smooth pavement gives way to the bone-jarring, tire-wearing gravel. So begins the road to the past.

Driving to Grasshopper requires caution, an alert driver, and quick reactions to what may wait just around the bend—horses, cattle, and occasionally elk or deer. At night the headlights may catch the reflective eyes of the silent-winged, stealth-footed predators—coyote, great horned owl, bobcat. As the road climbs, ponderosa pines begin to mingle with the scrubby junipers and oaks. At last the road forks, revealing a lush, open meadow enclosed by low, pine-covered hills and bordered on the east by Salt River Draw. A cluster of willows marks a spring; cows graze among the stone ruins slumbering in the meadow. Not far up the hill was the field camp, where once a hand-painted sign welcomed the traveler in Apache to Nas Tsuggi—Grasshopper. Today no sign marks the place that is Grasshopper, but traces of the distant and recent past are everywhere—ancient log and stone buildings, a decrepit and squeaky windmill, a battered stock tank. Circles of stones mark where campfires once blazed. Stone walkways that today lead nowhere once traced paths to cabins that rang with music and laughter. Everywhere there are pieces of the past—broken bits of pottery and debris from making stone tools. The remains of almost seven hundred years of human history are layered here in this isolated pastoral setting.

Through time, people of several different cultures came to Grasshopper—the prehistoric Native Americans that archaeologists label the Mogollon and others we call Anasazi, the Cibecue band of the Western Apache, and an international crew of twentieth-century archaeologists who came to learn archaeology and reconstruct Mogollon prehistory at the University of Arizona Archaeological Field School. The material traces of these people remain, surely, but there are deeper nuances as well. The people whose dramas of everyday life were played out at Grasshopper imbue it with a special and lasting gift; their spirit lingers.

How did Grasshopper get its odd name? Historian Will Barnes's *Arizona*

A few of the many painted pottery vessels from Grasshopper Pueblo: back row, left to right, Tonto Polychrome jar, Fourmile Polychrome bowl, Pinedale Black-on-white jar; middle row, left to right, Pinto Polychrome bowl, Cedar Creek Polychrome bowl; front, Cibicue Polychrome jar.

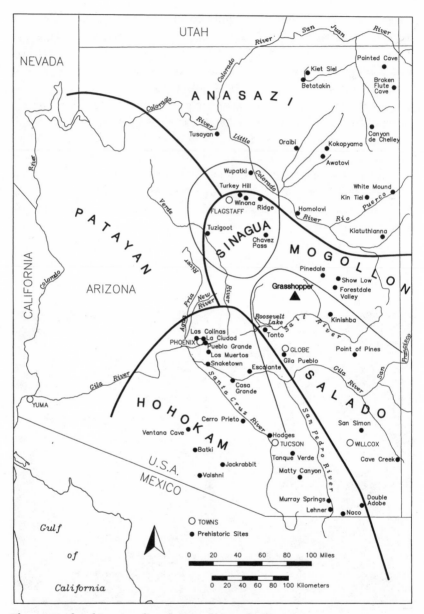

The principal prehistoric culture areas and sites of ancient Arizona

Place Names supplies one answer. The entry for Grasshopper reads: "Spring and camp on Fort Apache Indian Reservation, at head of Salt River Draw. So called as early as 1880 after a lame Apache . . . [woman] whom the Indians call 'Naz-chug-gee' (Grasshopper) from her peculiar limp. She had one short leg which caused the limp." Apache friends have told us a simpler story, that it is a place of many grasshoppers. We will never know what the Mogollon Indians may have called their home, for their language was not a written one, and thus no records survive.

For most of the 1300s, Grasshopper was a thriving Mogollon pueblo community, one of the largest in the mountains of central Arizona. The people of the land that would become Arizona developed ways of living that were structured by the natural landscape. Arizona has three natural zones, which geographers call provinces, that influenced prehistoric lifeways. The three major prehistoric cultures of the Southwest developed in these three provinces.

The basin-and-range desert of the south, where today are located metropolitan Phoenix and Tucson, is divided from the Colorado Plateau in the north by a zone of mountains running diagonally across the state. The Mogollon Rim, an escarpment varying in height from a mere bump on the surface of the earth to a steeply rising face, forms the northern boundary of this mountain zone. The Sonoran Desert of the basin-and-range province was home to the prehistoric culture we call the Hohokam. Hohokam, usually translated "those who have gone before," is a Piman Indian word literally meaning "all used up." Archaeologists who excavated the first Hohokam sites in the 1930s gave the culture this name.

The Colorado Plateau, a vast, uplifted zone stretching from the Mogollon Rim into Wyoming, dips into Arizona only in the northern part of the state. The Four Corners region where Arizona, New Mexico, Colorado, and Utah meet was home to people archaeologists call Anasazi. The word is a Navajo one, usually translated as "enemy ancestors." Another label for the Anasazi Culture that is becoming more frequently used is "Ancestral Pueblo peoples," and the Hopi people prefer to call the Anasazi of their homeland the Hisatsinom, meaning "our ancestors."

The Mogollon were the people of the mountains, the sweeping, rugged Transition Zone separating Colorado Plateau and desert. Of the three major prehistoric cultures in the American Southwest, the Mogollon is the least well known to archaeologists and the general public. Many unforgettable and photogenic monuments to Anasazi Culture exist, among them Chaco Canyon, Canyon de Chelly, and Mesa Verde. Since the turn of the twentieth century, these places have drawn professional archaeologists. Similarly, two decades of contract archaeology in metropolitan Phoenix and Tucson have made the Hohokam Culture extraordinarily well known to archaeologists and the public. But the ruins of the Mogollon Culture, secluded in the rugged and isolated country of outback Arizona, remain almost as unfathomable today as they were six centuries ago, when the Mogollon doused their fires, packed up, and left, never to return. Only the Gila Cliff Dwellings, a national monument hidden in the mountains of southwestern New Mexico, give a glimpse of the Mogollon to those who travel the narrow, winding road out of Silver City. In this book we give the reader a fresh, behind-the-scenes view into the prehistory of Grasshopper Pueblo, the Mogollon people, and their culture.

Mogollon people first came to Grasshopper in small family groups during the last quarter of the thirteenth century at a time when a severe and long drought—the so-called Great Drought—swept across the Southwest, driving people from their northern homes to seek better-watered land in the mountains. Coincident with the end of the drought and the abandonment of the Four Corners region around 1300, people came together at Grasshopper to build the pueblo community. Within a generation, they would expand the pueblo to nearly five hundred rooms.

Other prehistoric Indians also settled at Grasshopper. We think that some were related to the Anasazi, and others may have belonged to ethnic traditions as yet unrecognized in the artifacts of prehistory. These people faced a host of problems unique to their new home and new life-style: coordinating activities, developing the forms of social organization necessary for community living, and resolving the inevitable disputes rising from living, quite literally, one on top of another in a compact, two-story pueblo. Regardless of their success in achieving solutions to these problems, by 1400 Grasshopper Pueblo and the immediate region were abandoned.

Some three hundred years after the Mogollon and Anasazi residents of Grasshopper left, a new and unrelated Native American people, the Western Apache, moved into the Grasshopper region to hunt, gather wild plants, and tend garden plots in much the same manner as did the earliest Mogollon peoples. It was the Apache people who occupied the Grasshopper region at the birth of history. They named it, and today the land is theirs. The Apache presence left only ephemeral traces on the landscape, however, and we know little about their history and lives before the arrival of the United States Army, an organization concerned more with pacification than ethnographic description. It was not until the first anthropologists, most notably Gren-

The log cabin and stone house of the historic Grasshopper Trading Post

ville Goodwin, made their pioneering studies in the twentieth century that a reliable picture of Apache life before the establishment of the reservations emerged.

During the early decades of the twentieth century, a man by the name of Jacques (pronounced "Jockwees") ran a trading post at Grasshopper. A log building and another built of stone borrowed from the prehistoric pueblo ruin remain today to record his commercial dealings with the local Apache. Jacques's other major alteration of the local landscape was to build a dam across Salt River Draw at the northern edge of the pueblo ruin, creating a small pond. Sometime after 1919, this pond silted in and the dam was breached, cutting the present channel of the draw on the east side of the ruin. It was during these early reservation years that Grasshopper is said to have received its name. The Grasshopper Store closed in the early 1940s, when Apache families throughout the West End of the reservation were relocated to Cibecue as part of a program to foster education.

Today the Apache cowboy rides the mountain range in a way unchanged from that of a century ago. Grasshopper is the summer station for the cowboys mending fence and tending cattle in the Grasshopper district. In years past, they bunked in the rooms built and abandoned by Jacques, corralled their horses there, and draped cowhides over the barbed-wire fences to cure.

Even these traces of an earlier lifeway are disappearing rapidly. In 1970, when we first came to Grasshopper, the cowboy camp was alive with the whoops and hollers of dawn on the range. A weathered frame house south of the ruin on the meadow was the stockman's house, home of the boss man and his family. Now the stockman's house is vacant, and young Apache men are only part-time cowboys. The harshness, danger, and unprofitability of running cattle in the rugged terrain of the West End make it inevitable that this way of life will disappear, too. Only a few Apache remember cowboying on the West End, and fewer still remember Apache life at Grasshopper.

The Mountain Landscape

"We were essentially a mountain people, moving from one chain to another, following the ridges as best we could," one Apache has claimed, and his words may be taken to describe the Grasshopper Mogollon. Like the Apache who came after them, the Mogollon moved through the mountains "like the wind," as writer David Roberts describes it. Mountains sustained their way of life with an abundance of water, deer, turkey, mescal (agave), acorns, piñon nuts, and small garden plots for cultivating corn and beans. Mountains encouraged the people to develop hunting skills, keen eyesight, and physical endurance, and mountains provided a frame for viewing their world, evoking a reverence for the power and spirituality of the highest places. We must imagine that, as they were to the Western Apache, the mountains were even more than these things to the Mogollon. Anthropologists have come to recognize what Carson McCullers knew in *The Heart Is a Lonely Hunter*: "To know who you are, you have to have a place to come from." The land is critical to Native American self-identity, well-being, and spirituality. Quoting a Cibecue man, Keith Basso describes it well:

> Wisdom sits in places. It's like water that never dries up. You need to drink water to stay alive, don't you? Well, you also need to drink from places. You must remember everything about them. You must learn their names. You must remember what happened at them long ago. . . . You will walk a long way and live a long time. You will be wise. People will respect you.

We can best introduce the mountain world of the Grasshopper Mogollon as it appeared to field school students by presenting a panorama from the top of Grasshopper Butte. On the first Sunday morning of each field school season, Raymond H. Thompson, director of the Arizona State Museum, head of the

Raymond H. Thompson points out major features of the mountain landscape from atop Grasshopper Butte.

Department of Anthropology, and past University of Arizona Archaeological Field School director, led the newly arrived students on a field trip to Grasshopper Butte, two miles north of the camp. From atop the butte, Thompson introduced the new students to the wonders of east-central Arizona and the boundaries of the Grasshopper universe. At an elevation of 6,434 feet above sea level, Grasshopper Butte is only 250 feet shy of the highest point east of the Mississippi River, a comparison that never failed to amaze easterners. Waves of green, purple, and blue mountains rolled to the horizon, fading to an almost incomprehensible vastness and distance. We track here the mountains as Thompson did for the students, in a wide sweep across the horizon.

Beginning with the south, in the immediate foreground is a green strip of meadow surrounding the Grasshopper ruin, and, as Thompson would point out, slightly to the east and hidden by trees lies the field school camp. Continuing south along Salt River Draw, the pine forest grades into grasslands, juniper, and chaparral before the surface of the earth turns to rock and falls precipitously into Salt River Canyon. Farther in the distance are the Pinal Mountains, which supplied the pine logs for building Gila Pueblo and Besh Ba Gowah, prehistoric Salado pueblos in the mining and cattle town of Globe some 50 miles to the south.

Salt River Canyon, looking west toward the southern edge of the Grasshopper Plateau.

To the west, in the middle ground, the Sierra Ancha ("wide mountains" in Spanish) rises sharply several thousand feet on the other side of Cherry Creek, hiding cliff dwellings in its steep and inaccessible canyons. Beyond it are the Mazatzal Mountains, peaking to 7,888 feet. In the western foreground, an unbroken carpet of pines extends 4 or 5 miles to the ragged edge of the Grasshopper Plateau and suddenly stops where the cliffs of the Canyon Creek drainage begin.

The vista to the east is cut short by Spring Ridge, though tops of landmarks like Lonely Mountain locate the Cibecue Valley. To the north, the pine forests appear to undulate as they rise to meet the Mogollon Rim 12 miles away and more than 7,000 feet above sea level.

The sweeping view from atop Grasshopper Butte exemplifies the rugged terrain of the central Arizona mountains. Geological faulting and volcanic activity have created a heavily dissected landscape of high elevations and steep canyons. Narrow valleys divide this rugged land into north-south-trending plateaus separated by creeks. One of these is the Grasshopper Plateau, the uplifted, relatively level centerpiece of the Grasshopper region. The

Grasshopper region is a 320-square-mile area bounded by the Mogollon Rim on the north, Cibecue Creek on the east, Canyon Creek on the west, and Salt River on the south.

It was in this mountain setting that Grasshopper Pueblo was established and, as different people quickly settled there, grew to considerable size. For a time, the people prospered in their mountain land, developing new ways of earning a living and experimenting with new forms of organization and religion. Eventually, however, the mountains proved too harsh, and all of the people moved away. This book tells the story of that short time at Grasshopper Pueblo, in the mountain heart of Arizona, as revealed by thirty years of research by the University of Arizona Archaeological Field School.

The Mountain Mogollon

Archaeologists have found the Mogollon Culture to be an evanescent and ephemeral phenomenon, hard to classify and harder still to define and grasp. The Mogollon were elusive almost from the moment that archaeologists began to track their trail across Arizona and New Mexico. The Spanish word Mogollon, today pronounced "muggy-own," labels several natural features in Arizona and New Mexico. One of the first Mogollon sites excavated and reported was the Mogollon Village in New Mexico, and it was named after the Mogollon Mountains, which were in turn named for Juan Ignacio Flores Mogollón, a governor during the Spanish Colonial period of what would become New Mexico.

The Mogollon Culture was recognized and defined by Emil W. Haury when he was associated with the Gila Pueblo Archaeological Foundation of Globe, Arizona. Gila Pueblo was a private archaeological institution, and its name is renowned in southwestern archaeology. Archaeologists from Gila Pueblo defined several of the major prehistoric cultures of the Southwest, and Haury was intimately involved in this work. Although "Doc" Haury's name is probably most commonly linked with the Hohokam, it was Haury who first identified and defined the Mogollon Culture.

The first traces of the Mogollon were found during the summer of 1931, when Haury and Russell Hastings reconnoitered the mountains of central Arizona and western New Mexico for Gila Pueblo. During that survey, Haury noted a kind of pottery that he recognized to be different from that associated with the Anasazi Culture and from the red-on-buff pottery of the culture soon to be christened the Hohokam. Little further work was done at that time, however, as the Gila Pueblo archaeologists were deeply involved with the first excavations of Hohokam sites and the definition of that culture.

What Haury saw must have particularly intrigued him, however, for he returned to New Mexico several years later to excavate two pit house villages— Mogollon Village on a ridge high above the San Francisco River and Harris Village, located farther south in the Mimbres River valley. Haury's 1936 report on these two villages defined and named the Mogollon Culture.

In his report, Haury concluded that the Mogollon way of life was sufficiently distinct from that of Anasazi and Hohokam to merit the status of a separate, basic culture. This was a radical idea for the time, one not readily accepted by Haury's colleagues. Until that time, archaeological research had concentrated on the fascinating Anasazi ruins of the Colorado Plateau. All other archaeological regions were viewed as peripheral to the Anasazi Culture, which clearly dominated archaeological thinking, and the notion that other, independent cultures might have existed was treated with a great deal of skepticism.

For the next two decades, controversy and debate swirled around the Mogollon concept and played a major role in the selection of research topics and fieldwork locations. Haury established field schools in the mountains of east-central Arizona, first in the Forestdale Valley and later at Point of Pines, largely to address the questions of Mogollon antiquity and authenticity. Similar reasons compelled other archaeologists to investigate different areas. Among these were Paul Sidney Martin, who moved the Field Museum of Natural History's Southwest Expedition to the Pine Lawn–Reserve region of western New Mexico, and later J. O. Brew, who investigated the region just to the north with the Peabody Museum's Upper Gila Expedition.

An acceptable notion of the Mogollon Culture was not quickly forthcoming amid the continuing controversy, and it was not until 1955 that Haury's student Joe Ben Wheat was able to synthesize in his doctoral research the evidence accumulated by Haury, Martin, and a number of other archaeologists into a validation of the Mogollon concept. Although some anti-Mogollon sentiment lingered among its die-hard opponents into the 1960s, all the fuss over the Mogollon disappeared as rapidly as it had begun, not long after Wheat's dissertation was published. As the archaeology of the late 1960s and early 1970s attempted to investigate anthropological questions with scientific methods, the debate over the Mogollon was superseded by new controversies. In the 1980s a biennial Mogollon Conference was initiated to discuss research issues and results; by 1996 the ninth conference would celebrate sixty years of Mogollon archaeology. Few who attended recall the polemic and disputes that once embroiled the concept of Mogollon. To set the stage for reconstructing daily life at Grasshopper Pueblo, we summarize here what those sixty-plus years of Mogollon research have produced.

The Mogollon cultural sequence is generally thought to begin around A.D. 200. The origins of the people archaeologists recognize as Mogollon are poorly understood. For centuries, the Southwest had been occupied by small groups of people who made their living by hunting and gathering, along with farming in the more productive areas of the plateau and desert, and who moved across the land frequently in pursuit of this way of life. Until sometime around A.D. 1 or so, they did not make or use pottery containers. Archaeologists use the label "Archaic" to define this way of life, along with the period that it embraces and the people who practiced this life-style. Most archaeologists recognize a distinction between the life-styles of the early farmers and later pottery-making people.

These early farmers of the last centuries B.C., which is traditionally labeled the Late Archaic period, grew domesticated corn and other plants. The lack of pottery vessels, reliance on stone tools for grinding wild plant seeds, and other evidence suggest that they were less dependent upon corn than later peoples, and their life-style remained relatively mobile. We assume that the Archaic people of the mountains followed a seasonal round, moving from place to place to collect plants as they ripened and to hunt. In the summers, the people likely settled into larger encampments along the rivers to plant and harvest corn and other crops.

Around 200, plain brown pottery appears in the archaeological record. It was once thought that pottery, agriculture, and settled village life appeared as a package at about the same time. We now know that farming preceded pottery and that other aspects of technology, such as grinding equipment and hunting tools, remained unchanged. Pottery containers were rapidly accepted as a sturdy and secure means of storing corn and, somewhat later, as an efficient way of cooking corn and beans. With the introduction of pottery, the Mogollon become recognizable in the archaeological record.

The Mogollon sequence ends at different times throughout their homeland but concludes emphatically with the widespread abandonment of the mountains by 1400. Although this span of time is divided into numerous local phases, broad trends are grouped into three periods: Early Pit House, Late Pit House, and Mogollon Pueblo. These periods embrace patterns in architecture, settlement, and life-style that mark overarching periods of development in Mogollon history.

Over the many years that we have been studying the Mogollon at Grass-hopper Pueblo, we have found it convenient to use two ethnographic models to help portray Mogollon prehistory as we understand it. We draw these models from modern Native American peoples, the Western Apache and the Hopi. The Western Apache mirror many of the ways of adapting to the mountains that characterized the Mogollon for most of their existence. When the Mogollon learned improved farming techniques and perhaps much more from the Anasazi people with whom they mingled later in pre-history, they took on many of the traits and behaviors that have been de-scribed for the Hopi. We will return to the Western Apache and the Hopi as cultural metaphors for the Mogollon at Grasshopper Pueblo many times in the following pages.

The Early Pit House Period: 200–600

During this earliest recognizable era, the Mogollon life-style was essentially unchanged from that of the Late Archaic period, except for the addition of pottery to the inventory of household utensils. The earliest Mogollon pot-tery, like the first pottery elsewhere, was unpainted and made in simple shapes. We think it was designed primarily to store shelled corn, rather than for cooking or other purposes. Pottery was a great advantage over the baskets that had previously been used for storage. It was moisture-proof and safe from rodents. The Mogollon lived in pole-and-brush structures archaeolo-gists call pit houses. These houses were built over a pit excavated into the ground, often three feet deep or more, which provided warmth and security. These houses may have had gabled or arched roofs supported by posts, and they were usually entered through a covered side entryway. The earliest Mogollon houses were round or bean-shaped when viewed from above; later houses were rectangular.

From the size of villages, we think that the population was small, and we also think that the people continued a seasonal round that included farming, collecting, and hunting. There may have been frequent times of social unrest and economic uncertainty for the people. Many small pit house villages, such as the Bluff Village in the Forestdale Valley, were located on ridges and hilltops, suggesting a concern with defense and protection of people and foodstuffs. Some villages have a large pit structure, often called a great kiva, which suggests the importance of communal activities that incorporated the scattered households into a loosely integrated community. We are not sure what sorts of activities took place in these structures, but they probably included communal ceremonies designed to create spiritual bulwarks in times of stress.

We think that the people moved their residences frequently, according to the seasonal availability of different resources. In this way, households could compensate for the variable proceeds of hunting and wild plant gathering. Small garden plots of corn and beans augmented the diet in those isolated areas where cultivation was possible. We think that the Mogollon were less dependent on plant food cultivation than were their contemporary Anasazi and Hohokam neighbors, and in general this remained true for much of their history. The steep canyons, uneven rainfall, and fiercely cold winters of the mountains made corn farming a less dependable enterprise than it was along the wide, placid rivers of the hot deserts, although the mountains provided rich and sustainable hunting. For this reason, many of the ceremonial and social trappings of settled village farmers did not appear among the Mogollon until relatively late in their history. It was the mountains that dictated their way of life, which was far different from that of their neighbors.

The Late Pit House Period: 600–1150

Many patterns established in the previous period continued during this time, although the seeds for divergence were sown. The Mogollon continued to reside in villages of pit houses clustered more or less randomly around a great kiva. The number of villages and their size indicate that the Mogollon population of the mountains was far larger at this time than previously. Villages tended to be located on valley floors adjacent to farmland. This shift from the higher, defensible locations characteristic of the previous period suggests the growing importance of farming and the development of mechanisms for solving disputes and maintaining social harmony. The great kiva tradition developed still further, toward more formal architecture and diversity in form and size. The great kiva at the Bear Village in the Forestdale Valley, for example, was shaped like an animal, with four legs and a head. What would become a long-term pattern of coresidence—Anasazi and Mogollon people living together in the same village—was well established during this period. The developments among great kivas point to what was probably shared ceremonialism as the solution for forging independent households and people of different ethnic traditions into a cooperative, harmonious community.

In areas particularly rich in wild resources (especially favorable for farming because of soil conditions or water supply), larger populations and

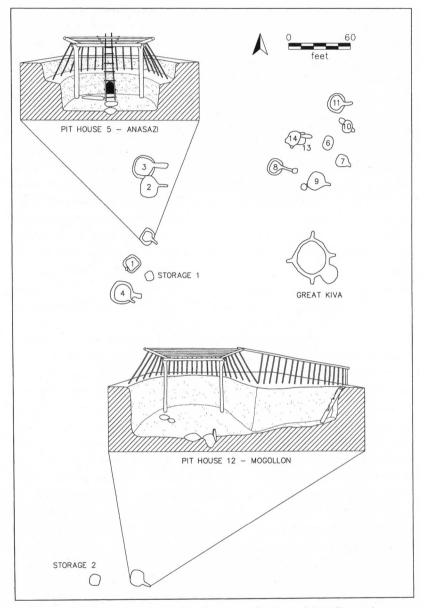

Bear Village, a Late Pit House period settlement in the Forestdale Valley, with enlargements of an Anasazi pit house and a Mogollon pit house.

longer village occupation were possible. The Forestdale Valley and Point of Pines are two such areas. In the less productive areas of the mountains, which were by far more extensive, the pattern of seasonal mobility continued to characterize the Mogollon life-style, which remained focused primarily on hunting and gathering.

In some parts of the mountains in the closing years of this period, the Mogollon lifeway began to diverge from its broad, fundamental pattern. In southwestern New Mexico, for example, the Late Pit House period ends around 1000 with the appearance of small, compact pueblos and the exquisite black-on-white pottery of the Mimbres Culture, the most famous of the Mogollon branches. The Mimbres Culture would thrive for almost 150 years. In the Arizona mountains, however, the life-style of the Pit House period continued longer.

The Mogollon Pueblo Period: 1150–1400

The appearance of pueblo architecture marked this period throughout the mountains, although there is regional variability in the time when pueblos appeared and in their size. Small masonry pueblos did not appear among the Arizona Mogollon until the mid- to late 1100s. The large, aggregated pueblo communities that were built earlier in the Mimbres Valley did not appear in the Point of Pines region until the mid-1200s, and only after 1300 did people in the Grasshopper region begin to build such large pueblo communities.

The period is further characterized by the elaboration of the mountain adaptive pattern and by the continuation of regional differences. The adjustment of dry-farming techniques to marginal environments tested the limits of agriculture in isolated areas, and hunting and gathering persisted among the seasonally mobile household groups scattered across the land. A period of environmental uncertainty and low rainfall—the Great Drought of 1276–99—confronted the Mogollon way of life with dramatically new environmental and social conditions. And here, at the beginning of the Great Drought, is when our story of Grasshopper Pueblo begins.

An Overview of the Prehistory of Grasshopper Pueblo

We use four developmental periods to frame the short prehistory of Grasshopper Pueblo and the sequence of major events in the occupation of the Grasshopper region in the 1300s. Each period represents about a generation, and the whole is punctuated by two major turning points—1300 and the 1330s—when striking changes took place.

The Establishment Period: 1275–1300

The story of Grasshopper Pueblo opens in a dramatic setting. A time of environmental deterioration and significant decrease in snow and rainfall, which archaeologists traditionally label the Great Drought, swept across much of the Southwest. It created particularly acute conditions on the Colorado Plateau and reached its height in the 1280s. We can think of this period as a Great Depression that severely affected the lives of prehistoric people throughout the Southwest, and those living in the Grasshopper region were not exempt from its widespread effects. The extensive economic, demographic, and social changes that we see in the mountain Mogollon after 1300 were responses, we think, to the strains and stresses to the fabric of their lives created by the Great Drought.

This time is characterized as one of small pueblo communities. Small settlements were scattered across the land, with a tendency to form communities composed of clusters of families around a central pueblo near soils suited to farming. Three sites where we excavated—Chodistaas, Grasshopper Spring, and Grasshopper Pueblos—were among these small pueblos. Because the small pueblo at Grasshopper was obliterated by later construction as the village grew, we must use Chodistaas and Grasshopper Spring Pueblos to represent the Establishment period of Grasshopper Pueblo. Chapter 2 describes this period and these pueblos.

The time was marked by dramatic and irreversible economic and settlement changes. The mountain adaptation of mobile families subsisting on hunting, gathering, and gardening that had characterized Mogollon lifeways for more than a thousand years continued until toward the end of this period, when it began to give way to increased farming and dependence upon cultivated crops. In the closing years of this period, the small pueblos would be abandoned for large, multistoried villages. The Aggregation period is named for this process of coalescing many small pueblos into single, large settlements.

We think that the archaeological evidence of bigger and more numerous sites reflects an actual increase in population. Who built these big villages, and why? On the one hand, "foreign" people evidently moved into the region to join existing communities. On the other hand, the Mogollon inhabitants of the region apparently decreased the seasonal movement that had characterized their life-style for so long and began to stay for increasingly longer periods in certain settlements. The Great Drought and associated environmental degradation affected the population of the Colorado Plateau profoundly. When the crops failed year after year, people were forced to move or starve, and these widespread demographic shifts spilled over into other regions. Anasazi from above the Mogollon Rim and perhaps people from the desert as well moved into the mountains seeking better-watered farmland. This movement of people into the mountains interrupted the traditional Mogollon pattern of household mobility. When families picked up to move after game or wild plants in their time-honored fashion, they often found other folks already residing at their traditional areas. In this way, the Mogollon came to occupy settlements throughout the year. This shift probably took place by the 1280s, at the height of the Great Drought.

The presence of more people in the region no doubt increased the competition for resources and created an atmosphere of social unrest and economic uncertainty. For families in small pueblo communities of the Grasshopper region, the threat posed by large, aggregated communities in surrounding regions would have intensified this competition still further. Social unrest may have reached the level of raiding. The three small villages in the Grasshopper region that we excavated had all been burned. It may be no coincidence that the Aggregation period was marked by the clustering of people into large pueblos. Defense and safety, as well as cooperation in economic and ritual activities, may have become paramount needs.

The Aggregation Period: 1300–1330

This period was marked by further social and environmental changes. At the same time that people on the Grasshopper Plateau left their small pueblos to settle at Grasshopper Pueblo and other large villages, with outsiders joining them, the Great Drought began to ease. In fact, snow and rainfall were significantly higher than normal during this period. The increased moisture for crops, sometimes as much as 25 percent above the average of 20 inches per year, meant bountiful harvests and more corn and other cultivated foods in the diet.

The trickle of change that had characterized population and settlement dynamics quickly became a torrent around 1300. All of the pueblos of the Grasshopper region dating to the 1200s together represent only an estimated two hundred rooms. But a mere generation after the eighteen-room Chodistaas Pueblo was burned and abandoned, there were almost two thousand rooms among pueblos in the area, and Grasshopper Pueblo was rapidly approaching five hundred rooms in size.

Construction on the three major room blocks of Grasshopper Pueblo began around 1300, and its growth accelerated rapidly. Patterns in the addition of new rooms for households suggest that Grasshopper grew by immigration of outsiders, followed by expansion of resident households. By the early 1320s the pueblo had grown to resemble the traditional Mogollon village layout of large room blocks enclosing open plazas.

The main portion of the village was divided by the original channel of Salt River Draw (before its historical period diversion by Mr. Jacques) into an East Village (Room Block 1) and a West Village (Room Blocks 2 and 3) surrounding three plazas. The southern corridor joining the two room blocks of the West Village was roofed by 1325. The three plazas were in use throughout this period of rapid growth. By the 1330s, one of the plazas, Plaza 3, was enclosed, roofed, and converted into the Great Kiva. We discuss these processes in more detail in chapter 3.

The Aggregation period at Grasshopper Pueblo is the one we know best, and we divide our discussion of it into the three major areas of human culture and behavior: ecology (chapter 4), sociology (chapter 5), and ideology (chapter 6).

The Dispersion Period: 1330–1355

Change did not cease for the people of Grasshopper Pueblo during these years. Further social and economic shifts took place as people adjusted to their new farming-dependent life-style in the face of a return to drought conditions of below-normal snow and rainfall. To compensate for what must have been the decreased productivity of their fields, the people founded a number of satellite villages in an attempt to bring more land under cultivation. This movement or dispersion of the population gives the period its name. More varied locations were occupied than in previous times, including the first significant use of cliffs and promontories for habitation, storage caches, and defensible lookouts. That many of the newly established pueblo villages were located on hilltops or other defensible locales hints at an ongoing concern with security. By this time, there were ten pueblos on the Grasshopper Plateau larger than thirty-five rooms, together representing an estimated two-thirds of all the rooms built in the region during the 1300s. Six of the pueblos had 35 to 100 rooms, three had 120 to 150 rooms, and Grasshopper Pueblo had reached its maximum size of 500 rooms.

The satellite settlements to which Grasshopper households moved during the Dispersion period were occupied only seasonally, at least in the beginning. The best-documented case of a satellite community is Canyon Creek Pueblo, a 120-room cliff dwelling excavated by Emil Haury in 1932. Red Rock House, another cliff dwelling not far from Canyon Creek Pueblo, was founded toward the end of this period. In the founding of these two satellite pueblos we see mobility as a time-honored response to stress. It also tells us much about the relationship of villages within the regional settlement system. We discuss the Dispersion period at Grasshopper and Canyon Creek Pueblo in chapter 7.

The Abandonment Period: 1355–1400

This period marks the final phases of occupation at Grasshopper Pueblo and its decline toward abandonment. Toward the end, Grasshopper Pueblo was occupied seasonally by some, year-round by others. Many families lived in low-walled room blocks that surrounded the main pueblo. Unlike the main pueblo, where several activity-specific rooms such as storage and habitation rooms were occupied by large households, all indoor household activities were compressed into a single room in the outliers. This compression of household activities suggests temporary habitation, perhaps during the summer, by smaller, younger families, while older households continued to occupy the main pueblo year-round.

Although it is unclear how many Grasshopper households moved temporarily to satellite villages such as Canyon Creek Pueblo and Red Rock House, it is certain that they and the rest of the people in the region eventually left. The abandonment of Grasshopper Pueblo was gradual rather than sudden. A small number of new rooms continued to be constructed after 1350, and additional household space was acquired through reoccupation of abandoned rooms. The last date is a tree-ring date of 1373, which is actually earlier than the year it was cut to serve as a roof beam.

The story ends in the 1300s. By 1400, all of the large pueblos of the Arizona mountains had been abandoned for full-time residence. The Mogollon had transformed themselves to the extent that they became indistinguishable, at least in the archaeological evidence, from the Anasazi. They had swapped their traditional small-group emphasis on mobile hunting and gathering supplemented by gardening for the life of the village farmer. The wild and free nature of the Mogollon life-style, so like that of the Western Apache, had changed irrevocably. They were, by this time, scarcely different from the other settled village farmers of the Southwest. Whether this change was for the better may not be appropriate for archaeologists to decide. Certainly this new lifeway was ultimately unsuccessful in the Grasshopper region, and the people moved on.

It is at this point in prehistory that archaeologists lose track of the Mogollon. The mountain Mogollon adjusted, changed, and disappeared from the mountain archaeological record as we currently know it. Their ultimate fate and who their descendants may be are unknown. Some of the Anasazi people living at Grasshopper, as well as some of the Mogollon, probably joined groups of ancestral Hopi people. Others may have moved to what is today New Mexico, becoming ancestors of the Zuni, the people of Acoma, or Pueblo peoples of the Rio Grande. But we do not know for certain, and we cannot therefore assign the Grasshopper Mogollon to a single historical period Pueblo people. We are certain that no Apache ever lived at Grasshopper Pueblo, for the Apache are an unrelated people who came to live in the Southwest after Grasshopper was abandoned.

An Introduction to the Grasshopper Story

One of the most intriguing things about Grasshopper, we think, is the similarity that the pueblo of Grasshopper shared with the field school at Grasshopper. Grasshopper has been abandoned, rediscovered, occupied briefly, and then abandoned yet again by different peoples over the course of its long history. Throughout this book, we place the major events in the history of the field school alongside the parallel events of prehistory. When we discuss the Establishment period, we balance it with a discussion of the founding of the field school at Grasshopper; the abandonment of the pueblo and the mountain region shares the same chapter with a discussion of the end of the field school, and so on. We hope by sharing these parallels to draw attention to the universal nature of human history. The processes and events that molded the history of Grasshopper Pueblo and the mountain Mogollon are fundamentally not that different from the problems and challenges we face today. And so the story that began in the pueblos begins anew in these pages.

2

The Establishment Period

All the time the sky had no clouds and no rain. The grandmothers could not remember summers more hot and dry. Many days the wind blew dust across the land and the smoke of many thousand burning trees darkened the sun. Our eyes stung and our throats hurt. At Grasshopper there was not much rain, but it was better there than on the plateau lands or down in the desert country. Grasshopper always had spring water for wild plants, for deer, and also for some corn.

So might the time of drought, the time of beginning at Grasshopper, have been remembered in the traditions of the people. The mountains of central Arizona form an immense, wild, rugged landscape often inhospitable to humans, punctuated intermittently by well-watered lands where corn could be grown without too great a struggle. It is paradoxical that only when this land began to languish along with the rest of the Southwest in history's worst drought did people begin to populate it more than sparsely. The curtain rises on our story during the Great Drought in the closing years of the 1200s.

But before this dramatic story of drought, migration, and relocation can be told, another tale must unfold—that of the discovery of Grasshopper Pueblo by archaeologists and the founding of the University of Arizona Archaeological Field School at Grasshopper.

Archaeologists Discover Grasshopper

The once-thriving Grasshopper Pueblo and other mountain pueblos lay abandoned and unknown for centuries. When the Western Apache came to live where once the Mogollon did, they rediscovered these abandoned pueblos. The Apache camped near ruins to harvest the sweet mescal, also called agave, that often grows there and to collect prehistoric stone tools and other useful materials for their own purposes. Other people did not learn of the ruins until much later. As we have seen, the mountain fastness of the Mogollon was not conducive to cattle ranching or farming, and because it was reservation land, it could not be settled by non-Indians. The first professional archaeologists to work in the Southwest around the turn of the century concentrated their efforts on the more spectacular ruins of the Anasazi country.

Despite the isolation of the ruins and the rugged character of the landscape, the region was briefly explored by some of the legendary archaeological institutions of the Southwest and some of its most famous archaeologists. Leslie Spier and Walter Hough were the first archaeologists to record the ruin at Grasshopper Store. Both visited the site in 1918, Hough during one of his many surveys of ruins in Arizona for the Bureau of American Ethnology and Spier during his survey of the White Mountains. Spier's note on what he labeled site 275 is brief: "There is a pueblo ruin at Grasshopper Spring west of Cibicue Creek, consisting of one large building divided by a flowing spring with numerous small buildings scattered around." Hough returned the following year to dig and collect artifacts.

Hough was remarkable for his tireless explorations of the ruins of east-central Arizona and also for the fuzziness of his field notes. His work at Grasshopper was no exception. His twenty excavations included trenches in exterior areas around the main ruin, in the large plaza, and in a number of rooms, only one of which has been identified by more recent work. His sketchy report, published in 1935, did little to advance our understanding of the pueblo.

Surveying to the south of Grasshopper along Salt River Draw, Hough also

The environment at Grasshopper Pueblo (middle ground) and the field school camp (in the trees at right).

visited a number of other ruins, including a large one that was probably what today we call Blue House. He also examined Red Rock House, a cliff dwelling on a lateral canyon of Oak Creek, but did not do much digging there.

The cliff dwellings of the Grasshopper region and the Sierra Ancha were first explored in 1931 by Emil W. Haury and Russell Hastings of Gila Pueblo. Haury returned to the Sierra Ancha in the summer of 1932, after his first year of graduate work at Harvard, to excavate Canyon Creek Pueblo, the largest cliff dwelling in the Grasshopper region. Cowboy rancher Slim Ellison's account in his book *Cowboys under the Mogollon Rim* conveys a sense of Arizona archaeology in the 1930s, along with insights into Haury's character, that can only be appreciated in his own words.

> Over the years we did a lot of packin for all kinds of parties. Learned a lot, too. It was about 1932 when I met Emil Haury at my dad's homestead, 20 mile east of Young. Haury was workin for an archeology outfit in Globe, called Gila Pueblo. I was to pack him and his crew of three men into some real ruff western country to explore and excavate some cliff dwellins. Before roads come into that country, my dad had a sled to haul in his hay and fodder from the fields, and later got a wagon. Well, when I arrived with 10 pack animals I noticed the sled—one of the first ways to move material—then the wagon, and the pack animals, and Haury's

Emil Haury dressed for fieldwork in the 1930s

trucks; then a one engine plane flew over. Some five ways of transportation, early and late, at one spot.

But that wasn't the only contrast—Haury was edjicated and smart. It had took on him, and I'd tell a hand Haury wasn't no softie, he was plumb full of vim and vigor, knew what he wanted to do, and was organized down to a gnat's eye. On the other hand, I had very little book larnin and was ruff and ignorant as a stomped lizard about most ever thing but handlin livestock and packin in ruff country.

Haury had been all over this part of country before on horseback lookin for some good ruin to excavate and had decided on one 10 mile east of Dad's place, up under a high rim on east side of Canyon Creek on Apache Reservation.

I was used to packin for cow outfits—beds in tarpaulins, seldom tents, Dutch ovens, spuds and beef. When he was ready to load up, thar was tents, gasoline lanterns, different kinds of tools, and chuck, and five gallon of gas for lanterns. I didn't like that. It's hard to pack and the darn stuff always leaks. We got started, followed cow trails, in some places none, jist headed toward the rims and found our own way.

The gas can sprung a leak and soaked the saddle blanket on the burro. It was about to blister 'im, and he was ringin his tail and faunchin around like a dog in a yaller jacket nest. He was on a steep hillside and not helpin any as I tried to unpack 'im.

About that time a mule's pack begin turnin to one side. Haury and one of his men got hold of 'im but couldn't make 'im stand still. Haury hollered down to me, "How do we make him stand still so we can fix the pack?" I ain't gonna tell what I said to him.

I took a canteen of water and washed the gas out of the hair on the burro's back and we finally got on our weary way.

About a mile farther on we scrambled up to the site. It was rather a nice place to camp. A bench, or shoulder, mashed out from the bluffs, level and large enuff for several tents, and 100 foot to one side a wonderful clear, cool spring bubbled out from under the Rim Rock. Nobody had messed things up, then. Tents was stretched and thing put in order. Rite here I messed up Haury's grub schedule. Always before in the country when a feller worked for anybody they furnished the chuck. I found out Haury had figgered to the ounce, even ever slice of bacon, and ever thing they'd need for a certain length of time. Jist the same, I got fed. I tied up a mule to wrangle on next morning, and hobbled out the rest. Haury and men was 10 miles from the nearest ranch and was alone with the ghosts and hoot owls. Many ole wild range cattle, b'ar, and lion, and prehistoric people had filled up on water at the spring where Haury and crew stayed. I gathered my stock and hauled for home 30 mile down on Cherry Creek.

In two weeks when I packed in more supplies for him, I found they'd been hard at it. Had uncovered 25 or so graves in the refuse dump and had 'em all cleaned up to photograph.

When I come back to move 'em out, they'd found a woman's skeleton in the cliff house with a sort of string skirt on and wrapped in a cotton blanket. They also had a baby in a cradle, and the pieces of a big pot that held 60 quart after it was put together at Globe.

I packed them and the loot out to their trucks. I can tell you them fellers worked hard, and at nite they lit lanterns and'd make out reports before hittin their soogans.

Years after this diggin, while pursuein the wild oxen high under the rims, I'd find a cliff dwelling, and thar'd be Emil Haury's mark—he'd been thar and took borings out of beams to git the age. I'll tell a man, Haury was a ramblin, scramblin, driftin, climbin, edjicated son-of-a-gun. You know, if our gover'ment could organize and work like Haury did that job, we'd have a sound, 100-cent dollar!

Another famous archaeologist linked with Grasshopper is Byron Cummings, the first head of the Department of Anthropology (then Archaeology) and director of the Arizona State Museum at the University of Arizona. Late

An Apache Sunrise Dance at Grasshopper in 1940

in his professional career, Cummings spent many years investigating the mountain pueblos of Arizona, including excavating and reconstructing Kinishba Pueblo, a similar site east of Grasshopper on the Fort Apache Indian Reservation near Whiteriver—but that story must be told another time. Cummings often took his students on field trips to interesting sites, and in 1936, perhaps inspired by Haury's work at Canyon Creek or possibly Hough's sketchy report of his work at Grasshopper, Cummings took his Kinishba field school students to Grasshopper. Photographs taken by Cummings indicate that he returned to Grasshopper in the early 1940s, where he attended an Apache Sunrise Dance, a girl's puberty ceremony. If Cummings ever excavated there, however, there are no records of such work. The rubble mounds concealed their secrets. Grasshopper was just another large, late pueblo ruin of the Arizona mountains, scarcely touched by archaeological hands and almost entirely unknown until the fall of 1962.

That year, as Raymond Thompson and his wife, Molly, recall, they camped in the flat south of the ruin where the abandoned stockman's house now stands. The mountain air's crisp coolness carried sounds of wind in the pines and whistling elk. They remembered with fondness many pleasant summers spent at the field school at Point of Pines on the San Carlos Apache Reservation, where Thompson began his career in archaeology and where he and Molly met. Point of Pines had only recently been abandoned for the Ringo site on the Coronado Ranch in southeastern Arizona. We cannot know if this camping trip and the archaeological promise it revealed was the impetus, but the following summer, after only one season at the Ringo site, Thompson moved the University of Arizona Archaeological Field School back to the mountains at Grasshopper. Certainly at Grasshopper, like Point of Pines, there were important archaeological opportunities for research and student training that simply were not available at the much smaller Ringo site. Thus, the summer of 1963 marks the beginning of the University of Arizona's seasonal occupation of Grasshopper, a thirty-year cycle of field school summers, each with its own community of staff and students and its own special character.

The Mountain Mogollon in the 1200s

Before the dawning of the 1300s, the Grasshopper region, like much of the central mountains, was inhabited by a small, scattered, and highly mobile population. The Grasshopper Mogollon, like the Cibecue Apache who came after them, relied on an intimate knowledge of the mountains, forests, and creeks to survive and prosper. The Mogollon lived in camps—short-term residences where people lived seasonally—or small villages, often near the soils best suited to planting. The cultivation of corn and beans, however, supplemented a heavy dependence on wild plant foods and the bounty of successful skilled hunters. Most of the mountain district, with its short growing season, uneven precipitation, poor soils, and limited opportunities for irrigation, is poorly suited for agriculture. Dependence on agricultural products was possible in only a few areas. The archaeological record of the Grasshopper region and nearby areas reflects these typical mountain conditions. We have found numerous specialized sites where hunting, butchering, and tool repair took place, indicating that hunting was an important activity. Wild plants were harvested and brought back to the home site for processing. The overall pattern is one of camps coupled with specialized places for processing resources that could not easily be brought back home. People moved to where the deer and the wild plant foods were plentiful; when they were gone, the people moved on.

It is possible that there are more sites in the Grasshopper region than we have yet found. The earlier sites can be difficult to see archaeologically, and some of the earliest are buried deeply. Yet we think that we have a fair representation of the range of sites in the region. And the small number of sites, their dispersion across the landscape, and the activities that were carried out tell us that the population was sparse and mobile.

The mountain people also forayed into the adjacent desert areas and onto the southern fringes of the Colorado Plateau. We know this from archaeological work along the Cholla-Saguaro transmission line corridor, which runs from the Little Colorado River in the north to Red Rock near Tucson and passes just 10 miles to the west of Grasshopper. People regularly traveled over considerable distances in search of particular plant foods and other resources. Mountain people traveled south to the Salt River and north all the way to the Little Colorado River. They always returned to the security of the mountains, however, especially during times of unrest.

Desert and plateau people also sought the rich plant, animal, and mineral resources of the mountains. The many different people who were attracted to the mountains did not often linger permanently, however. How do we know that people of different cultures used the mountains? There is considerable evidence for the surface mining in the mountains of steatite, a soft black stone also called soapstone. This stone was highly prized, particularly by the Hohokam, to fashion beads, pendants, and carved ornaments. The places where steatite was mined are scattered with Hohokam red-on-buff pottery, the distinctive Hohokam plain ware pottery that sparkles with mica, and Anasazi black-on-white pottery from the middle Little Colorado River area. Anasazi and Hohokam alike evidently journeyed into the mountains to obtain steatite, leaving behind their broken cooking pots and water jars. At mining sites dating to the early 1200s, no Hohokam pottery is found, and the Anasazi black-on-white pottery found at the quarries apparently was made on the Colorado Plateau north of Grasshopper. This is one of several bits of evidence suggesting that the direction of interaction shifted from an early focus on both north and south to an emphasis later in time on the Puebloan regions of the north and east.

We have speculated that the hunting prowess of the Mogollon with bow and arrow may have tempted them to raid desert and plateau farmers for food. Most of the evidence, however, points toward reasonably congenial relations with neighbors, such that the coresidence of peoples of different cultures was practiced for a thousand years. This joint use conditioned Mogollon and Anasazi, and perhaps Hohokam as well, to live and work together in relative peace. People of diverse cultures lived alongside the Mogollon in a number of villages. Walnut Creek Village on the Q Ranch Plateau west of Grasshopper and Bear Village in the Forestdale Valley represent Mogollon villages with architectural and ceramic evidence that indicates the peaceful coresidence of Mogollon and other people. The peaceful use of the mountains by people other than the Mogollon can account for many of the seemingly enigmatic patterns in the archaeological record.

The pattern we have described—one of isolated camps located near garden plots, occupied part-time by a mobile population of autonomous, related households living by their skills in hunting, gathering, and gardening—was long term, one that the Mogollon had followed for many hundreds of years. Rapidly, at least in archaeological terms, all of this would change. The Great Drought brought an influx of settlers. Their arrival created new constraints as well as fresh opportunities.

Drought, Abandonment, and Population Relocation

The Great Drought, which lasted from 1276 to 1299, brought a disastrous end to the century. Land on the Colorado Plateau that was marginal in the best years became useless for farming because of too little precipitation, lowered water tables, and erosion. Many parts of the Anasazi homelands, most notably the San Juan River drainage of the Four Corners region, were abandoned as people escaped to areas where the drought was less severe. The central Arizona mountains were a prime target for these displaced populations, for many springs and a high water table provided a more predictable water source than the arid Colorado Plateau. Families and groups of families packed up and trekked on foot, often hundreds of miles, to seek a better land and a new life. Evidence for population movement is widespread, but perhaps the best example occurred at the height of the Great Drought in the 1280s, when a group of Anasazi from the Kayenta region traveled south to live at Point of Pines Pueblo on what is today the San Carlos Apache Reservation. They brought with them their own unique styles of pottery decoration, house construction, and the varieties of corn they had grown in their homeland, all of which archaeologists nearly a thousand years later would recognize as different from those of the local Mogollon.

Shortly before the Great Drought began, three small pueblo villages sprang up in the area around Grasshopper. These were Chodistaas Pueblo, Grass-hopper Spring Pueblo, and one on the spot where Grasshopper Pueblo would later be constructed. Then, beginning in the 1280s, more people began to move into the Grasshopper region, as Anasazi from above the Mogollon Rim and others from the southern deserts fled the drought. At the same time, large pueblos were developing in the surrounding areas. This process of people coming together into large pueblo communities, labeled aggregation, took place throughout the Southwest but occurred later in the Grasshopper region than in neighboring areas. By this time, in the eastern part of what is today the Fort Apache Reservation, there were pueblos with as many as one hundred rooms, and north above the Mogollon Rim there were villages nearly twice that size. Population aggregation also was beginning in the cliff dwellings of the Sierra Ancha to the west, and still larger pueblos were being built in the Tonto Basin to the southwest. Ceramics and village layout indicate that many of these communities were occupied by indigenous Mogollon, as well as by people from the Colorado Plateau.

The migration of people into the Grasshopper region and the growth of aggregated communities outside of the region had two major effects on the local population. First, the mountain people could no longer move about freely. Their traditional pattern of residential mobility was interrupted, with the result that villages came to be occupied full-time, probably in the 1280s. Second, greater population density and the presence of displaced outsiders increased the competition for resources and created an atmosphere of social and economic uncertainty. For families in the small pueblo villages of the Grasshopper region, this competition would have been intensified by the presence of larger, aggregated communities in surrounding regions. Social uncertainty may have escalated into raiding. We excavated three settlements dating to this period: Chodistaas Pueblo, Grasshopper Spring Pueblo, and a third we never named. That all of them were burned suggests the possibility of widespread and recurrent raiding. Aggregation appears to have been, in part, a process that attempted to protect people and provisions from raiding. We do not know who the raiders were, although they obviously were aggressive. They may have been displaced Anasazi, local Mogollon who raided their neighbors because times were so hard, or other people who were newcomers to the region. In any case, it seems likely that raiding was fostered or intensified by the continuing drought, environmental degradation, and the resultant demographic consequences.

The shift from a seasonal to a year-round occupation probably happened at all the small pueblo villages in the Grasshopper region, even the settlement that would soon develop into Grasshopper Pueblo. Our best evidence of this time comes from the intensively excavated Chodistaas Pueblo, and we use it, along with Grasshopper Spring Pueblo, to represent the people and processes of the Establishment period. We now leap forward from the past to see Chodistaas Pueblo as it was excavated by field school students and staff.

Chodistaas Pueblo, 1976–1992

We celebrated Independence Day in 1976 in what may seem a curious fashion: clearing brush, logs, and stones and building a road to Chodistaas Pueblo. We were constructing a path that would lead us to a better understanding of the past. By the summer of 1976 we had been working at Grasshopper Pueblo for thirteen consecutive field seasons. We did not know everything about past life at Grasshopper, but we certainly knew a lot. One aspect remained a mystery: we did not understand the forces and the human

Excavation supervisor John Welch directs excavation of Room 13 at Chodistaas Pueblo.

processes that led to the building of what eventually became that five-hundred-room pueblo. Who built Grasshopper, and why? Just as important, what was life like in the early years, and how did it differ from later times?

We could not answer these questions by further excavation at Grasshopper Pueblo. The earliest rooms built there had been obliterated by later construction. The inhabitants robbed the walls of stone, so that only the foundation courses remained below the floors of later rooms. These walls and a few early potsherds were all that was left to tell the story. The rich artifact assemblages on Grasshopper room floors were late, left behind when the residents packed up and moved away for the last time. To understand this time it was necessary, therefore, to turn to other nearby sites that dated to the time of Grasshopper Pueblo's establishment and slightly earlier.

Sometime in the 1960s a pair of field school students seeking a little privacy and some lovely outdoor scenery happened upon Chodistaas Pueblo. They discovered a pristine site in a lonely setting, hidden among the junipers and piñon trees on the edge of a bluff overlooking a lush meadow, just about a mile north of Grasshopper Pueblo and the field school camp. In 1971 students in a University of Arizona class in southwestern archaeology were unable to find the site. They settled for mapping the artifacts scattered at the base of the bluff that had washed down from the hidden site above. Reid does not remember when he first visited Chodistaas Pueblo, but he does recall it as "a sweet little site that someday we had to explore." Eventually the site was relocated, and Chodistaas was targeted for excavation. In 1976 the time had come for this work, and Chodistaas proved to be perfect, far exceeding our expectations.

With the road blazed for trucks and equipment, we mapped the site, which we determined to have eighteen rooms and a large, walled plaza, and began excavating four rooms. We quickly reduced this number to two when we discovered that the rooms were much larger than those at Grasshopper Pueblo, and it simply was not possible to finish excavation of all four rooms in the remaining time that summer. Excavating those two rooms to the floor revealed a tremendously exciting discovery. Sealed below the fill of loose dirt, fallen wall stones, and trash were floors with a rich inventory of ceramic vessels, mealing equipment, and household tools, all blanketed by the charred roof beams and charcoal of an apparently catastrophic fire. We had found treasure, indeed, and it remained only to name our find. Because it seemed that almost every stone we overturned revealed one of the creatures, we named the site Chodistaas, which is the Apache word for "scorpion."

The field day begins at 6:20, when the bell rings across camp to sound the call: ten minutes to breakfast. At an elevation of 6,000 feet above sea level, it takes about a week for the human body to adjust to the altitude. On this July morning in 1983 we had been at Grasshopper long enough to accommodate to the altitude. None of us had adjusted to the seemingly constant lack of sleep or the early morning cold, however. Knots of staff and students gather in front of the dining room, huddling to catch the early sun's warmth. After breakfast, staff and students pack the trucks with water and field equipment and assemble their personal gear for a long day in the field.

Most leave early, preferring to hike to the site. Their mile-long trek ends with a breathtaking climb up a steep slope to the top of the bluff where Chodistaas sits among the trees. The first students to arrive peel back the black plastic that protects the rooms overnight. Spiders, field mice, and snakes take refuge under the plastic, often providing a little surprise that jolts their discoverer completely awake. Soon the air is alive with the grate of trowel on stone, the rattle of dirt being sifted through screens, and the good-natured ribbing that marks a pleasant field crew. German, Apache, and Spanish are languages heard at Chodistaas as often as South Carolina drawl and the clipped accents of the eastern seaboard.

Two University of Arizona Field School staff members and graduate students, Julie Lowell and Barbara Montgomery, are directing the excavation of Room 7. It will take the entire summer to complete it. We had learned that Chodistaas was unusual, perhaps unique; for all we knew, there was no other archaeological site in the region like it. The rich and detailed archaeological context we had discovered demanded meticulous care, and so we purposefully slowed down the work. The only real resource that we had was time, and we made the most of it.

Room 7 is big, measuring about 18 feet by 18 feet from inside wall to inside wall. Its size will further slow the pace of excavation. Today, Julie is directing the removal of tree-ring specimens, a back- and knee-breaking task. Each intact piece of burned roof beam must be painstakingly cleaned, removed, and stabilized with a mixture of gasoline and paraffin. Wrapped with cotton string and hung to dry, these "mummified" specimens swing from a nearby piñon tree like bizarre Christmas decorations.

This burned roof layer is black gold, more priceless than any artifact we will ever discover and well worth the pain of recovery. Charring preserved the roof beams, making it possible for tree-ring scientists to determine when the beams were cut and thus precisely when each room was constructed. Provided that the specimens are sufficiently intact and have enough outer rings, we can discover when Room 7 was built.

Room 7 at Chodistaas Pueblo, showing pots and other artifacts left on the floor
when the pueblo burned.

The substantial foundation courses of Room 7 are two stones wide. Originally the walls probably were no more than about 3 feet high. This solid
foundation supported a relatively flimsy superstructure. The roof was not a
typical pueblo roof, supported by enormous beams and thick with layers of
sticks and mud. Instead, it was more similar to a *ramada,* or shade construction, built with small poles of piñon and Douglas fir supported by
interior posts and covered with brush and mud. A typical pueblo roof covering a room the size of Room 7 would have to be supported by huge beams,
more than ten times the size of the poles being removed by Julie and her
students. The archaeologists will recover pounds of the burned roof mud,
which is called daub, fired to a ceramic-like hardness.

The charred roof beams hide another treasure. Chodistaas Pueblo burned
in a fire so sudden and so intense that the roofs of the rooms collapsed,
preserving under the fallen roof beams all of the household tools and containers that were in use on the room floors and that would not ignite. The
fire also apparently caused the village to be abandoned. The inhabitants of
Chodistaas did not salvage their pots and stone tools from the fire. These

things remained behind for Julie and a fascinated student crew to discover and study.

When all of the roof layer has been removed, this room will be revealed as a storage and manufacturing room. Room 7 lacks the features that characterize the habitation (living) rooms at Chodistaas Pueblo. There is no rectangular, slab-lined hearth for cooking or a slab-lined mealing bin for grinding corn. Instead, the floor of Room 7 is covered with a diverse array of ceramic vessels and other tools. There are also two clay-lined firepits, which apparently provided light and kept the occupants warm as they worked on various tasks. Room 7 served as a companion storage and manufacturing room to the adjacent habitation Room 4. Both rooms, along with two nearby storage rooms, were probably used by two related households.

Students must gingerly work their way around the thirty ceramic pots that cover the floor of Room 7, many of which are brown obliterated corrugated jars. These large pots, also called *ollas,* were used for cooking and storing food. The pots were smashed into many pieces when the roof collapsed, and the rims of the larger ones are clearly visible above the charcoal layer. Cleaning off the roof debris and soil from each pot and carefully removing it is another painstaking task. Scattered about the firepits in the center of the room are several decorated bowls, small jars, and a metate.

Later, the collection of almost three hundred whole vessels from Chodistaas Pueblo helped archaeologists to reconstruct patterns of population movement and interaction. Using characteristics of painted design, technology, and the chemical composition of the materials from which the pots were made, María Nieves Zedeño was able to distinguish ceramics made at Chodistaas Pueblo from those made elsewhere. Pottery made locally includes the pots that were used for domestic cooking and storage purposes. These include brown corrugated and plain ware pottery, a red-slipped corrugated ware called Salado Red, and a white-painted version of the latter. A corrugated ware with bold geometric designs in white paint, which archaeologists call McDonald Painted Corrugated, was probably brought into the Grasshopper region from the mountains to the east.

The decorated pottery is especially intriguing, and not only for the beauty of its designs. The black-on-white decorated pottery and two black-painted red wares, Pinto Black-on-red and Pinto Polychrome, tell a dramatic story of a mobile people. Except for two locally made vessels, the black-on-white vessels we found at Chodistaas Pueblo were manufactured to the north of the Grasshopper region on the Colorado Plateau. When people moved to Chodistaas Pueblo from the plateau country, they brought these black-on-white pots with them. We know this because the chemistry of the white clay—determined through the state-of-the-art technique of neutron activation analysis—is so different from that of the locally available clays, and it matches the composition of clays collected from the plateau. During the early years of occupation at Chodistaas Pueblo, people evidently continued to move back and forth between the mountains and the plateau. When people settled down to stay at Chodistaas Pueblo throughout the year, however, which happened relatively late in its occupation, they no longer obtained the black-on-white pots made on the Colorado Plateau. Instead, the people began to make black-on-red and polychrome pottery using the raw clays and other materials that were available in the immediate area.

During research for her dissertation, Barbara Montgomery would use the relative proportions of potsherds in the fill of the rooms and whole vessels on the floors to determine that, regardless of how it caught fire, Chodistaas Pueblo was ritually buried after it burned. The pueblo did not gradually fill up with washed-in dirt and trash as sites typically do after people abandon them. The dirt deposited inside the rooms was curiously thick with broken pottery and other trash. It would certainly be difficult for sherds to wash into rooms located on top of a hill, and only a few people camped temporarily at Chodistaas after the village burned, leaving little trash behind. Barbara reasoned, therefore, that after the pueblo burned it was deliberately covered over. People brought in trash from their refuse dumps as well as dirt to fill in the rooms and bury the pueblo in a special abandonment ceremony that we will never fully understand.

The road we built to Chodistaas Pueblo on July 4, 1976, served us well. It provided us not only with a picture of life as it must have been like at Grasshopper during the earliest years of its occupation but also with a wealth of unparalleled information that we never dared hope to obtain. We return now to the past, to use this priceless information to reconstruct ancient life at Chodistaas Pueblo.

Chodistaas Pueblo, 1263–1300

Sometime in 1263, a small group of Mogollon people with close ties to the Anasazi of the north decided that the high bluff, with its sweeping view of the countryside, was a good place to make a home. They began to build a small block of seven rooms, quarrying limestone and sandstone blocks and stacking them to build low-walled houses of dressed masonry. A large,

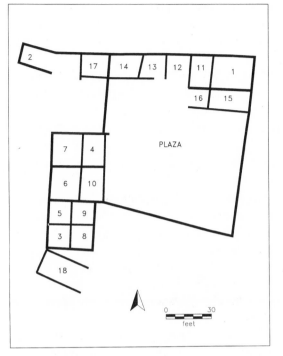

Chodistaas Pueblo

walled, open-air plaza provided space for outdoor activities and public ceremonies. Throughout the 1270s, people lived at Chodistaas on a seasonal basis, probably during the summer, working on the rooms even as they lived in
them. Where they went in the winter we cannot say for sure, but it surely was
somewhere to the north on the Colorado Plateau, if we can use the black-on-
white pottery that was made there as an indicator. Arborlike roofs of small
beams and brush sheltered the rooms during construction. The people may
have intended to build a permanent home with full-standing masonry walls
and solid roofs, but for unknown reasons they never finished. We do not
know by what name the people called themselves or their pueblo home or
even what language they spoke. Their language was not a written one, and
no reminders of it are left among the archaeological traces of their lives.

More people came to Chodistaas Pueblo between 1280 and 1285, during
the worst decade of the Great Drought. These people built the southern
room block that abuts the plaza. In the mid-1280s four storerooms were
added to the southern room block. Unlike other rooms at Chodistaas, these
storerooms were typical one-story pueblo rooms, not low-walled rooms.

They contained many storage pots, and each room had a mealing bin, but there were no cooking hearths. The construction of these rooms apparently marks an important event. This was the shift from living at Chodistaas on a part-time seasonal basis to permanent year-round residence. The storerooms were critically important, therefore, to provide secure storage for enough food to last through the winter and seed corn to plant the following spring.

Chodistaas Pueblo gives us a glimpse of household organization during the time when villages were small and the people who lived in them were related through blood ties and marriage. Each room block is composed of eight domestic rooms and one ritual room, suggesting the presence of two distinct social groups, each made up of individual households. We imagine that the four or five households that lived in each room block were related to one another. The distribution of artifacts on floors in the southern room block and the construction of rooms suggests that although two households shared a habitation room, a storage-manufacturing room, and a ritual room, each household had its own cooking hearth and storeroom for food.

The ritual rooms are Rooms 2 and 18, which have certain characteristics unlike those of the rooms in which people worked and slept. Each had an unusual orientation, offset from the other rooms and facing slightly south of east. Although we might suspect an alignment with a celestial or solar phenomenon, such as the solstice sunrise, we have discovered no convincing matches with any such events. Each room had an earthen platform or bench, one of which was plastered and one that had a stone facing. These features suggest the ritual nature of Rooms 2 and 18, but because the architectural features that mark later kivas at Grasshopper Pueblo are absent or less formalized, we call these early ritual rooms "protokivas."

The plaza was used for many different activities, but its most important function was communal and ceremonial. It served as a center for a larger, dispersed community formed of small camps and farmsteads. This larger community gathered at the Chodistaas plaza to carry out ceremonies, feast, and dance.

Sometime in the 1290s, Chodistaas Pueblo burned in a rapidly spreading, disastrous fire. The cause of the fire has always been a mystery, one that we are not certain we will ever solve. Was it accidental, caused by lightning or sparks from a cook fire? Or was the fire intentional, a deliberate action of raiders and plunderers? We do know how the occupants responded to the fire. Dirt and trash were tossed onto the fire so quickly that they smothered the still-burning timbers, preventing them from being consumed to ash. The household goods—all the pots, metates, manos, bone awls, and tools that represented the bits and pieces of their broken lives—were left, unretrieved, among the charcoal and ash. The people carried baskets of dirt, broken pottery, and trash from the nearby middens and covered over the remains of the floors and collapsed burned roofs, hiding all traces of the disaster. It is as though the pueblo home literally "died" (perhaps was cremated intentionally?) and was then buried.

And so the Mogollon left, abandoning the burned and buried Chodistaas Pueblo for a new life in a place just a mile away. They were among the first to merge with the people already living there to begin building what would become Grasshopper Pueblo. Its roof embers now cold, its buried rooms now hiding the secrets of its past, the ruined Chodistaas Pueblo began to decay and to become part of the archaeological record that we would study centuries later.

Grasshopper Spring Pueblo, 1270s–1300

Grasshopper Spring Pueblo is located a mile east of Grasshopper Pueblo, near a lushly vegetated spring at the edge of the same meadow that Chodistaas Pueblo overlooks. This clearly was an attractive place, to judge by the remnants of occupations ranging from the Late Archaic period to Apache, all located in the immediate vicinity. We are most interested in the occupation dated by tree rings to the late 1200s, contemporary with Chodistaas Pueblo. Eight rooms have been identified as having been built and occupied during this time. Because Grasshopper Spring was contemporary with Chodistaas Pueblo and located only about a mile away, it is all the more striking how different the two villages are. These differences tell us that the people who lived there belonged to separate cultural traditions.

We think that the little pueblo village of Grasshopper Spring was settled by a group of Anasazi. Several lines of evidence support this interpretation. There are, to be sure, some similarities in architecture. Like Chodistaas, Grasshopper Spring Pueblo is built of large, low-walled masonry rooms. It also has a ritual room, or protokiva, with an offset orientation and an earthen platform. The village layout is significantly different, however. Instead of room blocks abutting a plaza, Grasshopper Spring consists of isolated room blocks separated by open space.

There are similar contrasts among the ceramics. Whereas the decorated ceramics are much like those we found at Chodistaas, the corrugated pottery that was used for cooking and storage tasks is not. At Chodistaas Pueblo, the

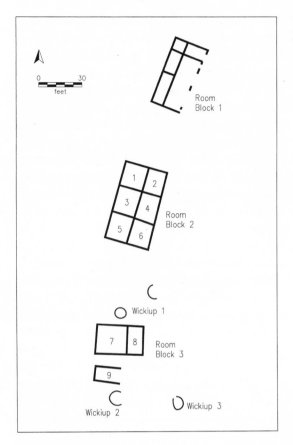

Grasshopper Spring
Pueblo

corrugated everyday ware was made from the brown-firing clays that were available locally and from which the Mogollon traditionally made their pottery. At Grasshopper Spring the corrugated pottery is orange-gray in color. Apparently local potters tried to duplicate the pottery of the Colorado Plateau that is made from the fine, gray-firing clays that are only found there. Evidently the potters of Grasshopper Spring took the brown local clays and by means of their firing techniques were able to create an orange-gray color to simulate the gray pots of their homeland. We find similar orange-gray pottery in the Cibecue Valley.

The cooking technology also is distinct from that used at Chodistaas Pueblo. In her research on fire features, Julie Lowell observed that the slab-lined cooking hearths that define the household at Chodistaas and Grasshopper Pueblos are absent at Grasshopper Spring. Instead, domestic cooking chores took place over a circular, clay-lined firepit. This difference suggests to us different domestic cooking traditions. Yet household organization seems to have been similar, with each household occupying two rooms, one habitation and one storage-manufacturing room. It is possible that the lack of slab-lined hearths speaks to the seasonal character of occupation at Grasshopper Spring Pueblo. The people may never have made the shift to full-time year-round residence as did the residents of Chodistaas Pueblo.

The most intriguing evidence for a cultural difference comes from Leon Lorentzen's analysis of projectile points. Using the relative size and weight of the points, he identified the spear thrower, or atlatl and dart, as the weapon used by the hunters of Grasshopper Spring Pueblo, instead of the bow and arrow used at Chodistaas and Grasshopper Pueblos. Rock art painted on the wall of a rock shelter, located on Cibecue Creek east of Grasshopper, supports the association of the atlatl with the Anasazi. Among a group of human figures rendered in the same style and technique, one is a man throwing a dart with an atlatl, and another depicts a female with her hair in the traditional butterfly of the Hopi maiden. Hopi believe themselves to be descended from Anasazi ancestors.

Together, this information leads us to believe that Anasazi people who maintained ties to the Cibecue Valley and also to regions farther to the

Human figures from a rock shelter on Cibecue Creek, showing a man (right) with an atlatl, or spear thrower, and a woman (upper left) with the traditional Hopi "butterfly" hairdo.

Leon Lorentzen, field school staff member and excavation supervisor, demonstrates use of the atlatl, or spear thrower.

northeast above the Mogollon Rim established and lived at Grasshopper Spring Pueblo at the same time that Mogollon people lived at Chodistaas Pueblo. There is no evidence that the interactions between people of these two cultures was anything but harmonious.

Yet Grasshopper Spring was, like Chodistaas Pueblo, abandoned, and also like Chodistaas it was burned. Unlike Chodistaas, however, the burial of rooms apparently did not take place within the context of an abandonment ceremony. The normal processes by which abandoned pueblos collapse and fill with washed-in dirt and debris gradually covered the Grasshopper Spring rooms. Because ritual burial of rooms was evidently not a tradition of the Grasshopper Spring people, this also may speak to cultural differences.

Prelude to Aggregation

The Grasshopper region at this time was a virtual melting pot, home as it had been for centuries to resident Anasazi and Mogollon people who also maintained ties to people of the deserts. For the most part, these people seem to have lived and worked together side by side in relative peace and prosperity. Life no doubt was similar at the small villages of Chodistaas, Grasshopper

Spring, and Grasshopper itself. It focused on family, with a firm foundation in spiritual life, and was heavily dependent on the wild plants and animals of the lush, yet rugged, mountain countryside. The people moved freely across the land, beginning to settle down more permanently as the 1200s drew to a close.

It was the long-standing tradition of cooperation between Mogollon and Anasazi that enabled Grasshopper Pueblo to be built. For whatever reason, the original small pueblo that was once at Grasshopper drew people from the surrounding country when they abandoned their own homes. The people who abandoned Chodistaas and Grasshopper Spring Pueblos joined people living at Grasshopper to found what would become the largest pueblo in the region.

Why did the people choose Grasshopper as the location to settle and build what would become a five-hundred-room pueblo? To Walter Hough, the reasons were obvious. He wrote, "The location of the Grasshopper sites was determined by the strong and permanent spring, the basin-like area in which water could be impounded, the excellent land available for cultivation, and the supply of wood for fuel, together with the good conditions for an abundance of game. Beams and stone for building and flint for various implements were also factors of advantage."

Those of us who have spent many summers at Grasshopper and have camped for at least a few days in every season of the year can add to Hough's list the smell of juniper smoke, the nightly light show of planets and stars, the brilliant sunsets, wind in the pines, and a mystical solitude found only in the Arizona wilderness. The mystery, if indeed any remains, is not why they settled Grasshopper, but why they left.

We think it probable that the Chodistaas people settled Room Block 3, joining the local folk living in Room Block 2 to form the West Village. The Grasshopper Spring people settled Room Block 1, which forms the East Village. Charles Riggs's research reveals architectural evidence pointing to this connection. For example, Room Block 1, like Grasshopper Spring Pueblo, does not enclose a plaza, and there are differences in the size and orientation of rooms that distinguish the East and West Villages.

The 1200s drew to a close with the abandonment of these little villages and a short journey to a new home and a new life. Our own journey to the past will lead us next to examine the forces of change that transformed forever these small, rural farmsteads and the families that they sheltered. But first an archaeological field school must be built, and a small community of university students and faculty must gather each summer for three decades. We look at these events next.

The Aggregation Period

Before we could understand why the Mogollon came together to build a five-hundred-room pueblo at Grasshopper, it was necessary for archaeologists to join together every summer for thirty years, forming a small, closely knit community devoted to understanding the past. We consider in this chapter the parallel processes of aggregation at the field school and the pueblo. The Grasshopper field school was many things. It was a field experience, a camp and its physical plant, and a school.

Grasshopper was an isolated archaeological field camp occupied every summer from 1963 until 1992. The field school experience was essentially one of total immersion in archaeology. There was no escape from Grasshopper, not even on the weekends. For seven days a week, one literally lived and breathed archaeology in the camp that was home as well as workplace. From 1963 until 1985, the field school lasted for eight weeks. The isolation, the lack of real-world intrusions and diversions, and the intensive schedule combined to produce an undivided focus on excavation, survey, laboratory processing, classification, and analysis. The camp setting, which by necessity demanded that every daily activity, from dining to showering, involve other campers, also encouraged the acquisition of the nonurban tradecraft essential to effective fieldwork anywhere in the world: self-reliance, knowledge of small-group social dynamics, and how to overcome the inherent perversity of a camp held captive by the whims of nature and mechanical devices. The field school was also a place to establish lifelong friendships and for many to meet those who would become husbands or wives. And the field school experience fostered for some students the critical revelation that archaeology was not to be their chosen field. For all, it was a special time to remember.

The Road to Grasshopper

To us, and we suspect also to the many others who loved it, Grasshopper is a kaleidoscope of images, a mélange of memories that deeply involve the senses and engage the heart. The first image is a vivid picture of the dirt road from Cibecue winding out of Spring Creek. After a long, steep hill, the road finally levels off below a cattle guard and fence that separate the white-faced Herefords of the Cibecue cattle district from those of Grasshopper. There the scrub oak and juniper give way to the pine forests of the Grasshopper Plateau. The exhilaration we felt upon leaving the hot urban desert of Tucson behind is as clear today as though it happened only yesterday. We always cut off the air-conditioning in the trucks and rolled down the windows to breathe the blessedly cool, pine-scented air. We can smell that air still.

From the cattle guard to the camp is 5 miles of flat, straight, dusty road through the pines and pastures. A few cows and their calves and mares and colts graze along the road. An Apache pickup might pass, returning to Cibecue with a load of firewood; otherwise, the last leg into camp heralded the isolation that would characterize life at Grasshopper for the next eight weeks. The road into Grasshopper, however, was never as rough as the one into Point of Pines, which Emil Haury remembers in his history of that field camp all too forgivingly. At its muddiest, the 10 miles of dirt and gravel from Cibecue to Grasshopper could never challenge a driver's skill and endurance like the 75 miles from San Carlos to Point of Pines.

At last, those last 5 miles seemingly endless to the archaeologist weary of the city and ready to begin a summer in the field, the road turns into the camp. After a brief tussle with a fiendishly formidable barbed-wire gate and a short uphill rise, we are in camp. The Grasshopper camp sits on a hill overlooking the pueblo ruin to the west and the cowboy camp that was once the Grasshopper Store. A fenced-in pasture for cattle and a motley mix of Apache horses and the occasional mule surrounds the camp. Those cows probably frightened urban students more than anything else the wild woods could offer. The nocturnal bellow of a bull, which sounds so peculiarly elephant-like, caused many a big-city student to wonder if the decision to go west for field school had been the right one. More than one washtub of laundry was lost to thirsty cows who failed to filter socks and underwear from water. And nothing is louder at 5 A.M. than a cow chewing meditatively on one's tent.

We increased the isolation of the camp still further by restricting access to the outside world. Students were discouraged from bringing an automobile and, once in camp, were prohibited from driving. There really was nowhere to go, and even if one tried, the slightest rain would transform the roads into deep-red, gooey, impassable mud. There was nothing we disliked more than hauling stuck vehicles out of that mess. More important, there was little free time. It was in such short supply that students and staff typically used it to catch up on sleep. The isolation of the camp, so far away from traffic, sirens, and all the racket and bustle of urban life, created a sense of aloneness that could be frightening. It was echoed by the slogan students coined one summer, styled after the trailer of a popular alien movie: "At Grasshopper, no one can hear you scream."

We shared the camp with assorted wildlife as well as cows. Although we often heard the coyotes singing at night, they were otherwise unseen. Squirrels and rabbits scurried everywhere, and occasionally deer would streak across the meadow, startling the cows. Ubiquitous and infinitely disturbing were the deer mice who took up residence in cabins. Their midnight forays among the hoarded junk food and their nests of squeaking, naked pink babies disturbed many a night's rest. Black bears, especially the young lonely ones that were newly on their own, occasionally wandered into camp. Although legend holds that the bears were simply following the irresistible scent of baking banana bread, more likely it was the less pleasant smells of our garbage dump that drew them. They certainly visited less frequently once we began taking garbage to the Cibecue dump. About once each summer, a rattlesnake would be encountered somewhere in camp. Spiders, snakes, and other assorted fanged creatures lurking beneath the outhouse seats were more a phobia than a fact. Of far greater danger was a fuzzy black-

and-green caterpillar that could drop from a tree on the wary or unwary alike or work its way into clothes or towels hanging on a washhouse nail. Reaction to this fuzzy creature ranged from simple itch to burning rash to serious systemic response, depending on the individual's sensitivity.

The Grasshopper camp, with its homey smells of supper and laundry soap, its friendly human voices, and its promise of hot showers and cold drinks, was an island of security in an isolated, dramatic, and sometimes frightening landscape. This was home for the summer; this was food, shelter, and comfort. To maintain that home while doing archaeology and teaching at the same time demanded we incorporate a seemingly endless series of chores into our daily routines.

The Grasshopper Camp

Each summer, after the field season had ended, the director wrote a report summarizing the work. In every one is a paragraph, actually a sort of secular prayer, describing the field camp. We quote from one report:

> The advanced science program was conducted at the University of Arizona's Archaeological Field School camp at Grasshopper, consisting of facilities designed to handle 20 students and a staff of 12. It includes a combination dining hall and kitchen, a large laboratory and lecture hall with a dark room, plus a number of cabins and house trailers for students and staff. These facilities were designed to require a minimum of staff time for maintenance, making it possible to devote maximum time to teaching and research.

As the facility that was designed to last ten years slowly approached thirty, this description's relation to reality diminished sharply. Although we might appreciate its subtle humor when back home in Tucson, in the field it seemed less than funny when daily effort, a great deal of hope, and occasionally prayer were required to maintain the physical plant. Something always needed to be fixed, and although many of those things could be ignored or put off for a while, others had to be attended to immediately.

The camp consisted of a number of essential and more-or-less interrelated systems. Water, originating from a well at the base of a windmill, was delivered by means of a submersible pump powered by an alternating-current electric generator, both of which were cursed in many languages over the years. It was necessary to pump water daily into a nine-hundred-gallon tank that in the early 1980s began to develop holes in the bottom. These were not

Men's dormitories at the field school camp in 1964. Today, all that remains are the rock walkways.

small holes (some were about the size of a quarter), and they had to be plugged with pieces of inner tubing held in place by an intricate arrangement of wedges and counterbalanced levers. These water-retention devices had to be reset at the beginning of each summer and fine-tuned throughout the season. In time, the entire water system became a masterpiece of jerry-rigging, of which a few of us are justly proud.

There was no electricity, except what was generated on the spot. Until the mid-1970s, electricity was produced by a World War II–vintage, 2-kilowatt, direct-current generator inherited from the Point of Pines field school. The Kohler generator, its only printable name, was left in place over the winter because it was the size and weight of a small European automobile. During the cold winter, its interior cavities inevitably would be converted into rodent homes, most notably for deer mice, a use incompatible with the production of electricity during the summer. The electricity this machine generated ran only the lights, an old-fashioned wringer washing machine that was eventually decommissioned, and the evaporative cooler for the kitchen. If we wanted to show slides during a lecture, then a staff member or two would retrieve the AC generator from the well and set it up outside the laboratory-lecture hall. As the vintage Kohler generator became harder to repair and demand for electricity increased, we converted to a 4-kilowatt AC generator. The Kohler was deposited in the Arizona State Museum, and its present disposition is unknown. Our muscles sometimes twitch in remembrance, nonetheless.

The sound of the generator was peculiarly comforting, and it ran each evening until 10:30 P.M. and the beginning of quiet hours. Staff members became particularly sensitive to the sound of the healthy generator engine and anxious when it coughed or sputtered, which often happened right when the mashed potatoes were being prepared for supper. The new AC generator, although an improvement, was still a heavy, ungainly machine without handles that had to be moved each year from Tucson to Grasshopper and back again by no fewer than four strong persons.

Not dependent on electricity were two old propane gas refrigerators and one gas freezer, essential appliances for storing food for twenty-five to thirty people in the middle of the woods. The gas tank for these appliances was located near the shed housing the Kohler. Some of our most truly frightening moments at Grasshopper involved watching lightning strike progressively closer to that tank during summer's intense thunderstorms. Lighting the gas appliances, along with the two gas water heaters, at the beginning of each season provided the only real hazard to setting up camp. It was not unusual for a bearded staff member to get lightly singed, and even the beardless could get a quick curl to the lashes.

Initially, showers of dubious warmth were provided by filling 55-gallon drums with hot water, which was mixed with cold and delivered by garden sprinkler heads. Students were forbidden on pain of death to touch the knobs that blended the bath mixture. The vagaries of weather and staff energies often meant a product more frigid than tepid, however. Eventually the director realized the possibilities of a direct-delivery system, and the luxury of hot showers became reality.

There was, of course, no indoor plumbing. The gender-specific outhouses were two-seaters that, mercifully, required little maintenance and whose walls became an outlet for creative writing. In the early days of big field camps, the outhouse locations were moved each summer in the interest of sanitation, and the backhoe was used to dig a new hole and move the structure. This proved an occasional opportunity for experimental archaeology, as once or twice we "witched" to find a site that avoided bedrock.

Obtaining, preparing, and serving food represented another delicate and energy-demanding camp system. Initially we followed the old schedule that had been established at Point of Pines, going to town every two weeks to buy groceries and supplies. In 1976 we realized that someone actually went into town about every week and thereafter always bought groceries weekly. A staff member drove the 55 miles into Show Low—"the town named by a turn of a card"—to pick up the food ordered on the previous week and to spend a day shopping for camp, staff, and student items. The "Show Low run" was one of the most arduous tasks the staff faced. In addition to picking up food and supplies, there were always multiple errands to fill the needs of a staff and student body kept isolated from pharmacy, grocery, and laundromat.

Finding antique replacement parts for recalcitrant machines and faulty plumbing, dropping off tires to be fixed at the garage, and filling prescriptions were common tasks. Less frequently, sick folk had to be shepherded through a visit to the clinic at the Navapache Hospital, or the gasoline drums might have to be filled, and even once or twice a pet dog or cat—smuggled illicitly into camp against the director's wishes—had to see the vet. There were also years when the Show Low run included doing the staff laundry. The shopping became such an onerous, grueling, all-day ordeal that we eventually decided to have a student buyer shop each week for student needs. The reward for this heroic effort was usually a chance to visit the Dairy Queen. Needless to say, ice cream was always in short supply at Grasshopper.

When the Show Low run returned to camp, usually in the late afternoon, the bell summoned everyone in camp to transfer the groceries from the tightly packed pickup truck to the refrigerators, pantry, and the root cellar, an old-fashioned, semiunderground cooler for fruits and vegetables. In the early days of the Grasshopper field school, when the field staff numbered three to five people, including the director, the absence of even one person for the grocery run meant an appreciable reduction in supervision.

Cooks were very near the top of the camp hierarchy, often more important than the director. A series of outstanding cooks proved the dictum every wise camp director knows: a field school runs on its belly, and the cook can make or break the field season. With great fondness, we recall the specialties that bulked up our hips and soothed our spirits—Ila Mae McFarlin's cherry cream cheese pie, Ruth Scoggin's red velvet cake, Daphne Tuggle's handmade tortillas, and Valerie Griffin's home-baked breads.

Pairs of camp aides, who typically were young men, were an invaluable component of the well-tuned and well-financed camp of the early years. Their primary responsibility was to wash dishes and do the heavy cleaning and fetching for the cook. But they were also the principal camp gofers, daily pumping water into the tank, filling the 55-gallon drums for showers, burning garbage, cleaning the showers and outhouses, and stocking the latter with hot lime and tissue.

The most demanding tasks by far involved setting up camp at the beginning of summer and dismantling it at the end. A week or so before the field school began, the staff would pack four or five long-bed pickups with equipment and supplies in Tucson and head 180 miles north to Grasshopper, where the first week was spent bringing up all the systems after a winter of rain, snow, freezing cold, wind, and the effects of the horses, cattle, and rodents who occupied the camp. Buildings had to be made ready for the occupants, and rat pellets removed from cabins, trailers, and appliances. During the last decade, an entire, exhausting, seven-day week was required to set up camp—even though we had an experienced, youthful, and energetic staff.

Vandalism beginning in the early 1970s quickly halted the previous practice of closing camp by simply locking the doors and boarding up the windows. After a number of years in which we hid the kitchen gear behind milk lugs filled with hundreds of pounds of ground stone artifacts, all equipment was stored either in the old Cibecue jail—rented from the Cibecue police for five hundred rounds of .38-special wadcutter ammunition—or stuffed onto pickups and hauled back to Tucson. We grew more expert at packing those trucks than almost anything else we did at Grasshopper. Closing camp at the end of the season could be done with student assistance in about three days. In the early years, however, the camp-closing routine also included coating all the buildings with shingle oil. Setting up, maintaining, and winterizing a deteriorating field camp took an inordinate amount of staff time, energy, and knowledge of gas and electrical appliances, internal combustion engines, plumbing, basic roofing, and elementary carpentry.

We have tried to give the reader a taste of the maintenance and logistical tasks required simply to live at Grasshopper before even beginning to contemplate the needs of research or teaching. But, like Emil Haury's understated description of driving the 75 miles of road into Point of Pines, even this account falls far short of conveying the true nature of these efforts.

In the Field at Grasshopper

The work day began at 7:30 A.M.. For the staff, this meant loading trucks with all necessary field equipment and supplies for the day's work, an especially onerous duty when we were working at sites other than Grasshopper

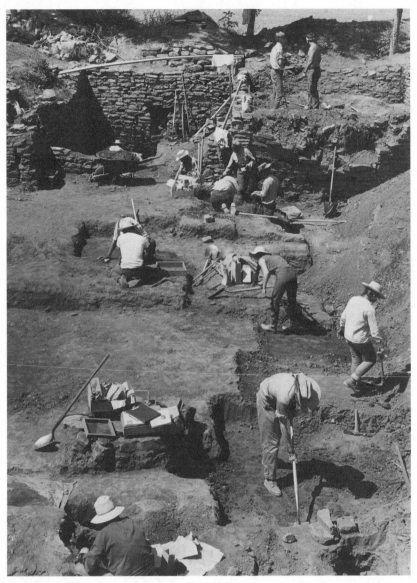

Excavation of Plaza 3—Great Kiva in the West Village of Grasshopper Pueblo

Pueblo. Inevitably, we forgot something. Water—to drink and to dampen down the excavations—was always at the top of the packing list. In the good old days, when we worked at the main ruin and had full-time cooks, coffee break at 9:30 always included baked goodies, breakfast leftovers, and pots of coffee and Kool-Aid carted down to us by the camp aides. Those same cooks served hot meals at lunch that all too often induced a need for immediate sleep. Later, finances and health considerations caused us to pare down coffee break and lunch alike.

Work ended around 4 P.M. Afternoons were usually reserved for laundry, sleep, and writing field notes or letters home, but as the season wore on the mounting laboratory work often intruded. After dinner, which was usually served outside under the sheltering trees, there often were lectures by staff members or visiting scholars. The day ended with quiet hours at 10:30 P.M.

On Saturdays the field day ended at noon, and Sundays were days of rest. These times served to renew and revive body and spirit. A staff member often would lead a hike to one of the many cliff dwellings or other pueblos in the region. A trip to Canyon Creek to swim was a rare treat. Even at Grasshopper it always seemed that Monday morning came too soon.

The daily schedule was orchestrated by The Bell. This length of cast-iron pipe was hung outside the kitchen and rung by banging upon it energetically with a solid metal rod. Its deep bong sounded several times each day. At 6 A.M. it woke the sleeping camp, and at ten minutes to mealtimes it warned us to clean up tools and wash up. It announced breakfast, lunch, and dinner, and once a week it signaled the arrival of the Show Low run. Everyone knew that when the bell rang at other times it was an emergency of some sort. Different cadences marked each event. The bell was rung slowly for wakeup, slightly faster for ten-minute warnings, and rapidly for meals. The staff grew artful and often creative at ringing the bell. We all grew to hate that sound, and as the summer lengthened and we grew increasingly weary, we learned to sleep right through it. Inevitably, students stole the bell each summer. It was hidden away and eventually ransomed, often by ice cream, in a requisite and legendary ritual. In the interim, staff made do with inverted buckets and spoons.

There were a few pleasures unique to the field school experience, such as volleyball. After supper, the energetic would convene on the dirt court to play until dusk. More real injuries, orthopedic and emotional, occurred on the volleyball court than anywhere else in this wilderness of forests and chaparral. Hiking was the next most common pastime. The meadow at sunset was a popular destination, as was Grasshopper Spring, just a mile away.

Slightly farther was Martinez Ranch, an abandoned Apache wickiup and the site of an early experiment in ethnoarchaeology. Saturday nights were for gathering at the campfire circle or for a boom box–powered dance in the dining room, or maybe both. We will never forget one Saturday night when a Volkswagen bus of lost campers wandered into camp seeking directions. We have often wondered what they must have thought on encountering a group of archaeologists happily boogeying to the Rolling Stones in the middle of nowhere.

The Grasshopper School

The Grasshopper field school was a research and teaching experience that was unparalleled. Scores of young archaeologists were trained there, carrying the knowledge they acquired at the pueblo in the pines to universities, museums, and other institutions across the United States and the world. The archaeological context in which they trained was uniquely rich, providing extraordinary learning experiences, and the research they produced was

Field school students sort pottery behind the laboratory-classroom building.

often innovative. The Grasshopper field school also provided a venue for understanding something of the history of American archaeology. For thirty years the field school operated in the current methodological and theoretical milieu. This research context changed over time in radical and unforeseen ways. Few other research programs can provide such a window into the history of our discipline.

The Early Years: 1963–1965

Raymond H. Thompson directed the Grasshopper field school for three field seasons. Thompson's move from the Ringo site to Grasshopper returned the University of Arizona Field School to the Arizona mountains where it had been based since the 1930s. In a sense, the first years at Grasshopper were an extension of the Point of Pines work, and both carried on the Arizona field school tradition established many years before. This rugged, no-nonsense, hard-working ethic that valued fieldwork was exemplified by Emil Haury. Haury spent his formative years as an archaeologist with Dean Byron Cummings at the University of Arizona. This experience taught him many things, one of which was that students could not automatically learn proper archaeological field technique on their own. Simply going through the motions of fieldwork, regardless of how many times the exercises are repeated, does not ensure that the puzzles of prehistory will be resolved. Haury knew that students can no more pick up appropriate archaeological field techniques on their own than they can acquire the procedures for transplanting organs from one human to another from books.

Haury also knew that archaeological fieldwork had to be taught in an actual field situation. One of Haury's outstanding recollections is of his graduate days at Harvard, where in the basement of the Peabody Museum there was a sandbox for teaching excavation techniques. He expressed great relief at being exempt from this requirement because of his prior field experience in the Southwest. Emil Haury was a fieldworker, knew fieldwork to be essential, and established the field school to teach field techniques of data collection.

Archaeological field schools may once have been a means of getting inexpensive student labor for a project, and for some low-budget projects it was the only source of labor. At the University of Arizona, however, there is no evidence that university credit was used to lure cheap student labor, although it was always a means of partially compensating them for their efforts. Instead, the essential role of the student was to pursue research into prehistory as part of the training and education of future archaeologists. For undergraduate participants, fieldwork was as integral to their education as the laboratory was to the physical and natural sciences. For graduate students, fieldwork provided an opportunity to develop and execute a thesis or dissertation research project under the close supervision of experienced faculty.

And so the Arizona field school tradition moved to Grasshopper, as it had once been focused on Forestdale, Kinishba, and Point of Pines. As the camp buildings rose at Grasshopper, the character of Grasshopper Pueblo slowly emerged. The first investigations were exploratory, designed to determine the distribution of rooms and artifacts across the site (no small feat, given its size), the range of construction techniques, and the dating of rooms. Trenches dug by hand and by backhoe were cut through the alluvial clays of the main ruin to identify the characteristics of the subsurface deposits.

The mundane and unique features of this five-hundred-room pueblo yielded to persistent archaeological probing. The general layout of the site emerged. There were three major room blocks in what became known as the main ruin and a number of smaller room blocks, called outliers, surrounding the main unit. There were three plazas, and a roofed corridor provided the sole access to the pueblo. Archaeologists found a series of masonry ovens and a deep trash deposit on the east side of the pueblo. They discovered that many rooms held arrays of abandoned tools and facilities. The Great Kiva, a huge ceremonial structure, was excavated—a major undertaking requiring a backhoe and dump truck donated by the Museum of Northern Arizona. Underneath the kiva lay a plaza where numerous burials were interred. Among these was the burial of an adult man, labeled Burial 140 in the list of excavated burials. This individual plays a pivotal role in our interpretation of ceremonial and social organization at Grasshopper.

By the time the directorship of the field school was turned over to William A. Longacre in 1966, the main features of the site were understood reasonably well. The stage was set for new directions in research that Longacre would provide and for a different kind of archaeology.

In the 1964 season a new tradition was established at Grasshopper. For eight years, from 1964 through 1971, the field school participated in the Advanced Science Seminar Program of the National Science Foundation. Under Longacre's direction, field school training was enriched considerably by this sponsorship.

Probing the Past: 1966–1978

In 1966 Longacre took over as director of the Grasshopper field school and immediately stamped the research program with a distinctive imprint. Following trends that characterized American archaeology as a whole, research at Grasshopper began to focus on more specific problems than characterizing the pueblo and determining when it was occupied and by whom. Questions of broader anthropological interest were asked (how the ancient residents of Grasshopper related to their environment, to each other, and to other people), and there was an explicit concern with scientific procedures. Archaeologists phrased questions about the past as hypotheses to be tested in the archaeological record of a particular site or region. A site such as Grasshopper became a laboratory. For us, these were also our years of introduction to Grasshopper and our own training—salad days that we remember fondly.

The Advanced Science Seminar Program of the National Science Foundation, which sponsored the field school until 1971, was a graduate student program, designed by Emil Haury and Raymond Thompson, that set the format and agenda for the teaching component of the field school throughout its thirty-year history. Excavation, survey, and laboratory work were augmented in the evenings with lectures by visiting faculty and archaeological professionals. Students were required to keep daily notes on their excavation, to write a summary report describing and interpreting their excavation unit, which usually was a room, and to design and complete an analytical report on a research problem. These heavy academic requirements combined in the final weeks with finishing excavation and laboratory work to make long, hard days and short nights. Exhaustion as well as sadness accompanied the end of the field school.

Deciding where to excavate in this large pueblo ruin became a major obstacle to overcome. Toward this end, a project was initiated in 1967 to map, measure, and determine the construction sequence of rooms so that an effective sampling strategy could be designed. The idea of sampling in archaeology—limiting excavation rather than completely excavating an entire site and deciding which rooms to excavate in the case of a pueblo site—had replaced earlier notions. It was thought that because archaeologists could learn as much about a site by a representative sample as through digging the whole thing, some portion of an excavated site should be left unexcavated and preserved for the future. There was the additional advantage that sampling required less labor and was, therefore, less costly. Rooms and the artifacts on the occupation surfaces (floors, rooftops, and surfaces underlying floors) bounded by rooms became the principal units of analysis.

Research also expanded to focus on aspects of Grasshopper Pueblo that would become central to our understanding of its construction history, use of space, activity organization, and ritual life. It also expanded to include other sites in the region. David Tuggle led an intrepid crew of surveyors through the catclaw and manzanita in the first systematic survey of the Grasshopper region. Supported by a National Science Foundation Grant, the survey became his dissertation of 1970. In 1976 work began on Chodistaas Pueblo. At Grasshopper excavation shifted away from focusing solely on pueblo rooms to investigating outdoor activity areas, including the plazas, along with mapping the entire site and collecting a sample of artifacts from outdoor trash areas. Plazas 2 and 3 were explored between 1974 and 1976. One project focused on some of the first rooms built at Grasshopper and another on household organization, and a number of the outlier rooms were excavated. There were experiments with computerized cataloging programs, different kinds of dating techniques, nonexcavation techniques for locating sites, and much more. The graduate students who staffed the field school during these years sweated and agonized to produce an astonishingly productive array of dissertations, and much of this research we discuss here.

When J. Jefferson Reid took over directorship of the field school in 1979, he inherited the remarkably enriched understanding of Grasshopper Pueblo that had accumulated in seventeen years of research. We knew just how large, complicated, and intimidating the ruin was. We had learned the kinds of techniques that worked best with such a site. We had discovered a tremendous amount of information. It was time to put it all together.

The Final Years: 1979–1992

Reid introduced some radical changes to the research program and maintained other aspects. Archaeology was shifting direction once again. The enthusiasm of the 1970s had given way to a more realistic appraisal of what was and was not possible at Grasshopper and to a concern with rigorous techniques for understanding how the archaeological record was formed and how to use it to interpret the past.

One of the first major discoveries was that the sampling program initiated under Longacre's direction was simply unworkable. Grasshopper rooms were unlike those in the Hay Hollow Valley excavated by the Vernon field school, where pueblo sampling was first used. They were twice as big. A fill of mountain clay rather than wind-blown sand meant harder, slower digging and dreadfully slow screening. Perhaps most significant, the number of artifacts recovered from any single room was staggeringly disproportionate. In contrast to the number of potsherds found at entire sites in the Hay Hollow Valley (34,000 from Carter Ranch Pueblo, 26,000 from Broken K Pueblo, and 19,899 from the Joint Site), a single room at Grasshopper, Room 164, yielded 15,563 potsherds. Indeed, 5 pueblos excavated by the Vernon field school—Broken K, Joint, Mineral Creek, Hooper Ranch, and Table Rock, a total of more than 150 excavated rooms—together yielded fewer potsherds than the 17 excavated rooms at Chodistaas Pueblo.

The astounding quantities of material found at Grasshopper required equally staggering amounts of time to wash, catalog, sort, and classify, and there was little financial support for these phases of study. Therefore, Reid decided to slow the intensity of sampling, focusing on rooms that could answer our questions without inundating us with material. In all, we excavated 105 rooms, giving us a 20 percent sample of Grasshopper Pueblo.

Another change was Reid's decision to stop excavating human burials in response to concerns of the Apache people. After 1979, whenever a burial was encountered, it was left in place undisturbed. We continued to probe the character of other archaeological sites in the region, recognizing that we could not completely understand what happened at Grasshopper Pueblo unless we also grasped the bigger picture. We returned to Chodistaas Pueblo for intensive excavation, worked at Grasshopper Spring Pueblo, and investigated several other sites less intensively. Survey of the region to locate sites became an intrinsic component of the research, and students rotated between excavation and survey crews.

After years of Longacre's bachelor directorship, Grasshopper became a family camp again as daughter Erin Reid joined the field school group. The tree house in front of the director's cabin, built for Raymond Thompson's young daughters, returned to active use.

The Grasshopper field school ended in 1992. In 1974 Longacre and Reid wrote, "It has taken us 10 years to get to this point in our research endeavor and we anticipate another decade before we can finish our work at Grasshopper." That the field school endured almost twice that estimate is testimony to its limitless potential. The University of Arizona Field School was moved to a different venue under a different director.

Everything we know about Grasshopper prehistory comes from the Grasshopper field school, particularly the hard work of student participants, graduate student researchers, and the Cibecue Apache, who helped us to understand Native Americans of the past and the present.

We leave the Grasshopper field school to address the parallel aggregation of humankind that took place there almost seven centuries ago. Why did the Mogollon come to Grasshopper and build a five-hundred-room pueblo there? What were the forces drawing people to this particular time and place?

Aggregation at Grasshopper Pueblo

Aggregation of Mogollon people at Grasshopper Pueblo and throughout the Grasshopper region began around 1300 and lasted for a little more than a generation, ending around 1330. Rapid growth at Grasshopper, like the explosion in population throughout the Arizona mountains, coincided with significantly greater than normal snow and rainfall, which provided welcome relief from the previous quarter-century of drought. It also provided—for a brief time—security and freedom from hunger. The town that was Grasshopper Pueblo must have seemed little short of paradise to people who had traveled long, seeking land to farm.

The 1300s mark a special time in Mogollon prehistory when the mountains of Arizona experienced the largest year-round population ever, and most of the Mogollon lived in communities of one hundred to a thousand rooms. This final and dramatic struggle to settle the Arizona mountains can be glimpsed in the ruins that surround Grasshopper—Point of Pines, Kinishba, Tundastusa, Q Ranch, the cliff dwellings of the Sierra Ancha—as well as at Grasshopper Pueblo.

We have seen that continued immigration of outsiders and the establishment of villages in areas surrounding the Grasshopper region increased real and perceived threats to the smaller communities of the Grasshopper Plateau and Cibecue Valley. Burned villages hint at a breakdown of the time-honored customs of joint use and probably demonstrated vividly the inadequacy of a settlement system composed of small, dispersed, and vulnerable households.

The reshaping of territory and rescheduling of procurement patterns required a renegotiation of resource procurement rules and social relations. One result was increasing emphasis on food production to accommodate the growing need to manage dwindling resources and heightened conflict.

The Cibecue Valley, which had been occupied intensively during the 1200s, was abandoned around 1300 as aggregation began on the Grasshopper Plateau, although the fertile valley fields continued to be farmed by people living at Blue House Mountain and Black Mountain pueblos on the eastern flank of the plateau. Abandonment of the well-watered Cibecue Valley for the upland Grasshopper Plateau, which lacks permanent surface water, clearly was not an effort to seek a better climate for agriculture. In making the move, the inhabitants of the Cibecue Valley, who we believe were Anasazi immigrants from above the Mogollon Rim, brought with them a more sophisticated dry-farming technology and a stronger commitment to corn cultivation.

We think that the formation of large villages on the Grasshopper Plateau was initially in response to threats against people and provisions. But soon the growing population forced the development of new solutions to mounting social problems. New forms of organization were needed to maintain cooperation and to settle disputes among households of similar and dissimilar cultural traditions. The community decisions would be made by ceremonial societies and their leaders. The importance of the Arrow Society at Grasshopper Pueblo, as we will see later, is consistent with aggregation under conditions requiring defense.

How did Grasshopper Pueblo reach its maximum size of five hundred rooms? What were the processes of its internal construction and growth? Most important, what did the pueblo look like when it was alive with people and sounds?

Grasshopper Ruin and Pueblo Growth

Grasshopper Pueblo, covering about 30 acres and once the largest community in the region, is now a masonry ruin. All that remains are rubble mounds, well hidden under a cover of walnut, juniper, and squawbush that rise from the valley floor along Salt River Draw and dot the surrounding low hills. The rooms are concentrated in the three room blocks of the main ruin and further distributed in ten small, outlying room blocks and scattered groups of rooms. The spring and the shallow pond it occasionally forms lie to the north of the ruin, across the modern road from the cowboy camp and hidden in a thicket of cottonwoods and willows. On the surrounding hills are outlying room blocks constructed of the same type of low-walled masonry found at Chodistaas Pueblo. Low mounds of trash are found south of the main ruin.

Three to seven separate core construction units began the settlement that would become Grasshopper Pueblo. We think that the original inhabitants

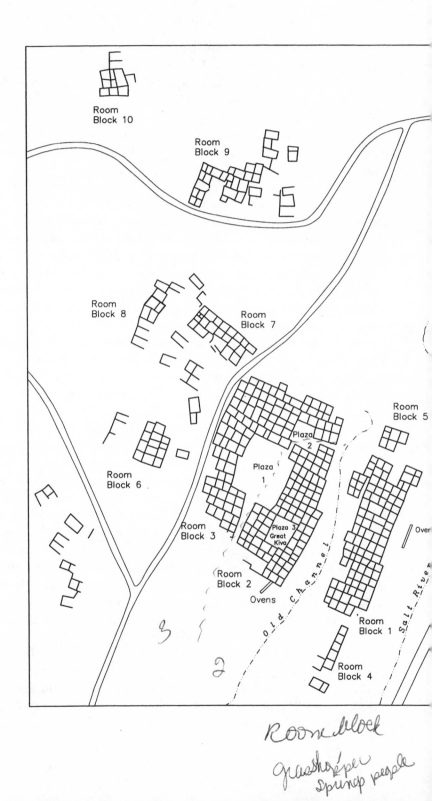

Room Block 10

Room Block 9

Room Block 8

Room Block 7

Room Block 5

Room Block 6

Plaza 2

Plaza 1

Room Block 3

Plaza 3
Great Kiva

Over

Room Block 2

Ovens

Old Channel

Salt River

Room Block 1

Room Block 4

Room block

grasshopper
Spring people

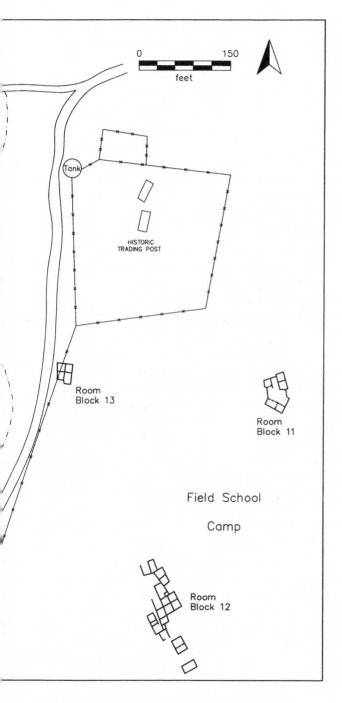

Grasshopper Pueblo, showing the location of the historic trading post and the field school camp.

of the locality built the twenty-one-room core unit of Room Block 2 and that the five-room core unit that started Room Block 3 was built by households moving in from Chodistaas Pueblo. Room Block 1 was probably founded by households from Grasshopper Spring Pueblo. The construction sequence of the main pueblo indicates that it grew steadily, although haphazardly, for a generation, first through the addition of multiple rooms housing large households and later through the construction of single rooms as these founding households expanded.

By the early 1320s the pueblo had achieved the typical Mogollon village plan of rooms enclosing an open plaza. The main ruin was divided by the old channel of Salt River Draw into the East Village (Room Block 1) and the West Village (Room Blocks 2 and 3). There were about one hundred ground-floor rooms in each of these room blocks and three plazas and a Great Kiva.

Unlike Chodistaas, the main pueblo at Grasshopper was built of full-standing, masonry-walled rooms one to two stories high. Because the average room size is so large (144 square feet), the five-hundred-room Grasshopper Pueblo is comparable in total floor area to a contemporary thousand-room ancestral Hopi pueblo on the Colorado Plateau such as Homol'ovi.

Grasshopper builders were skilled stonemasons. They preferred to use the tabular pink sandstone that outcropped nearby but occasionally resorted to the more irregular gray limestone forming the low hills surrounding the pueblo. Exterior walls were made of well-shaped pecked stone blocks laid on a mud mortar held in place with thin stones as chinking. These well-crafted exterior walls, like the rougher stonework of the interior walls, were covered with a facing of mud plaster. The rectangular doorways were low, forcing the passerby to stoop going through them. As the pueblo grew, rooms were added, abandoned, and changed in function. No longer functional doorways were sealed with masonry blocks. We think that the majority of rooms were entered from the roof hatchways.

Roofs on rooms within the main pueblo were used just like interior room floors. They were therefore built solidly to support continuous foot traffic and a full range of household activities. Two primary beams of ponderosa pine, each about the diameter of a medium-sized telephone pole, crossed the long axis of the room. The beams were anchored securely in the walls. On these supports were placed fence-post-sized secondary beams of juniper or piñon, spaced about a foot apart. Split juniper shingles placed on top of the secondary beams were in turn covered with grass and a thick layer of mud. A hatchway was constructed with flat stones shaped to fit the opening and often notched to secure a ladder. Most rooms, whether one or two stories, were entered through the roof by means of these hatchways.

A roofed corridor opening into Plaza 1 from the south and another corridor opening into Plaza 2 from the east were the only entrances into the West Village. There were no exterior doorways. Any doorways that may have been left open during room construction to make it easier to haul and stack the stones were sealed when the work was completed. The rooms around the plazas were entered through ground-floor doorways and ladders leading to rooftop hatchways. The outside rooms and the East Village were entered by way of ladders that could be pulled up at night or any time danger threatened. A person casually sitting on the rooftops of the two-story part of the West Village could see anyone approaching the pueblo and monitor the movement of friends and strangers alike. All of these features signal some concern with village security.

Daily domestic activities as well as public ceremonies took place in the plazas. We borrow Byron Cummings's words, which portray the plaza at nearby Kinishba Pueblo, to give a sense of the sights, noise, and bustle of the Grasshopper plazas. He wrote, "One can let his imagination have full play and conjure back the scenes of that great court of long ago. He can [en]vision its work and its gossip, its wails of sorrow and its shouts of laughter, its dances and its processions, and listen for the echo of its chants and prayers."

Around 1330, Plaza 3 was roofed and converted into the Great Kiva, a large ceremonial building that served the Grasshopper community and the satellite communities throughout the region. Plazas 1 and 2 continued to serve as daily gathering places and the dance ground for public ceremonials. Smaller ritual rooms or kivas were located throughout the pueblo. There were no formal cemeteries. Most of the children were buried below the floors of rooms and most of the adults in the plazas and trash areas.

Grasshopper would have been an impressive pueblo community, especially to Mogollon families accustomed to living in small settlements of only a few related households. Approaching from the south, it would have appeared to span the width of the valley, and the two-story section of the West Village would have seemed twice as high because of the sudden rise in the bedrock ridge beneath it. A person entering the pueblo had to walk through the long, narrow confines of the corridor, which was architecturally more like a dark tunnel than a welcoming hallway. As the corridor opened into the village, however, the visitor would be inside the sunlit Plaza 1, and the community would come alive with the raucous noise and activity of everyday domestic life—grown-ups chatting, children yelling, cook fires smoking, and hungry dogs skulking along the perimeter in search of scraps. The welcoming smell of juniper fires would mingle with the stench of refuse. On religious days, the plaza margins and adjoining rooftops would be filled with spectators from throughout the region, as this ancient amphitheater resonated with the sights and sounds of ceremonies for health, harmony, and especially for the abundance of plants and animals.

Archaeologists will never know how the people of Grasshopper Pueblo would talk about their everyday life to us today. Certainly it would be far richer and more personal than the story archaeologists piece together from the careful study of artifacts. Nevertheless, we hope that our interpretation of their life according to ecology, sociology, and ideology, described in the following three chapters, would ring familiar to them.

4

Grasshopper Ecology

Many snows made the ground good for planting, and every summer after the
longest day the hard rains came. There were huge clouds in the north. The sky was
dark and quiet before the thunder and the lightning and the rains. The rains came
like a waterfall. They filled the creeks and covered the farms with water and new
soil. Our hearts lifted when the rains came. It was a time of joy and for prayers
of thanks. Everyone had plenty of corn and beans and squash, and there were
many deer.

Sitting around the fire, the old men and women of Grasshopper may
have recalled the end of the drought in much this way. After a
quarter-century of little rain, hunger, and what seemed a ceaseless
quest for food and safety, the rains brought a time of relative security
for the mountain Mogollon and those who had joined them in the
drought years. The growth of the pueblo we call Grasshopper coincided not only with a period of higher-than-average precipitation
but also with an increased focus on agriculture, and we think that

the timing of these events was not purely coincidental. The people of Cho-distaas and Grasshopper Spring Pueblos, like generations of mountain Mo-gollon before them, had lived by hunting deer and turkey, gathering acorns, piñon nuts, and juniper berries, and cultivating small plots of corn, beans, and squash. The first people to settle Grasshopper Pueblo followed this same life-style. Within a generation, however, they would completely change this way of earning a living to become village farmers fully committed to and totally dependent on corn agriculture for their livelihood. Just as quickly, they would be forced to leave the mountains to pursue the new life of a village farmer elsewhere.

What forces could have brought about these sudden and dramatic changes? The standard explanation for the adoption of agriculture is that hunter-gatherers, when fully informed of the benefits of corn agriculture, automatically discarded their bows and took up digging sticks. The best explanation we have found to date is more complicated. The process of adopting intensive food production at Grasshopper, which took place long after it had occurred in most of the Southwest, illuminates the general pro-cesses that operated in the distant past, when corn was first introduced into the American Southwest from Mexico.

In this chapter, we explore the processes by which the Grasshopper folk became full-time farmers, along with other topics that form the core of ecology—human adaptation to the environment, defined in its broadest an-thropological terms. How people make a living is determined in part by their environment and technology, although the range of adaptation to any en-vironmental context is wide. We humans are infinitely creative in this re-spect, as in so many. The Anasazi, the Hopi, and the Navajo all inhabited the Colorado Plateau, for example, but made their living in different ways.

This uniquely human interaction with the environment is what makes an anthropological "landscape" different from "land." Landscapes are contex-tualized environments that reflect the meanings that people have given to nature and the land, symbolize their history, religion, and worldview, and embody their self-definitions. For example, certain mountains of the Colo-rado Plateau country define the Navajo world and are associated with cre-ation stories. They are a constant reinforcement of Navajo beliefs and iden-tity. The landscape is the spatial and material manifestation of the relations between people and their environment. It is a testament to its history of use, aesthetics, social traditions, and decision making.

Food, shelter, clothing; these are the fundamental human needs we dis-cuss here. We examine first the modern environment around Grasshopper

Pueblo and ways in which the prehistoric environment may have differed. We explore how people at Grasshopper made a living, focusing on hunting, wild plant gathering, and farming. Included in this section are aspects of the economy not related to obtaining food, such as manufacturing and trade. Because technology plays such an important role in mediating between people and their environment, we discuss the tools of everyday life. In addressing the transformation to full-time farming, we present the processes that compelled the people of Grasshopper to take up agriculture so intensively and some of the reasons why they were forced to give up this life-style for greener fields elsewhere. Dependence on agriculture had unexpected consequences, and we discuss these as well. We close with some metaphors for Grasshopper subsistence at different points in time, borrowed liberally from the ethnographies of Western Apache and Hopi peoples.

The Environment of Grasshopper Pueblo

As we saw in chapter 1, the Grasshopper Plateau is a relatively flat, uplifted plateau that lies between higher elevation and more dissected country to the north and lower elevation, equally rugged land to the south. Toward the Mogollon Rim, which lies about 15 miles north of Grasshopper, the country rises progressively in a series of unnamed mountains capped by Chediski Peak at 7,460 feet above sea level. To the south, the plateau is drained by Salt River Draw and Spring Creek. Elevations there drop to 4,000 to 5,000 feet as the country slopes toward the Salt River. This hot desert country contrasts with the cool high forests, and the bottom of the Salt River Canyon can feel like hell itself on a summer day. Canyon Creek marks the abrupt drop in elevation on the west, and to the east, toward the Cibecue Valley, there is a similar drop in elevation.

This diversity in landforms meant that many different animals and plants were available to the Grasshopper people for food, construction and craft materials, and fuel. Three major groups of plants occur in the area around the pueblo, and others could be reached easily by traveling only a short distance. At the higher elevations, the vegetation is ponderosa or western yellow pine, with small stands of spruce and Douglas fir on the cooler slopes. These trees supplied long, straight timbers to roof pueblo rooms. Ponderosa pine forest, dotted with an occasional alligator-bark juniper or Gambel's oak, dominates much of the area immediately around Grasshopper. Open clearings with a few juniper seedlings, squawbush, and grasses punctuate the

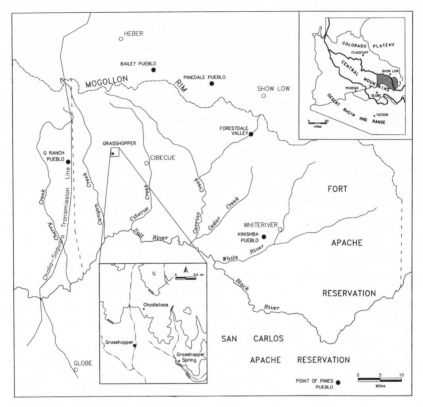

The Grasshopper region

forest, creating a parklike atmosphere. Except for the squawbush, which provides tart, lemony berries, there are few edible plants in the ponderosa forest. There is, as you might suspect, abundant fuel wood.

More important economically was the evergreen woodland association, composed of juniper, oak, ponderosa pine, and piñon. These trees dominate much of the Grasshopper Plateau and are found on the stony ridges that surround the pueblo. Construction and fuel wood, piñon nuts, juniper and manzanita berries, deer, and other game animals abound in this plant community.

Meadows and grasslands interrupt the pine forests around Grasshopper and become more prominent to the south. The grasslands developed on deep soils that lack rock outcrops, which not unexpectedly were favored farmland. Edible plants in this community include grasses, herbaceous plants, and cactus. We remember the meadows around Grasshopper more fondly as a favorite destination for sunset walks.

To the south, the evergreen woodlands of piñon, juniper, and oak grade into dense chaparral brush as elevations descend to the Salt River and the plants of the desert. Anyone hiking, fishing, or rafting the Salt River on a sweltering summer day would never suspect that a hike of just 18 miles up Salt River Draw would lead them to forests of tall pines. Agave or mescal and cactus of many species thrive on canyon slopes at these lower elevations.

Where the natural vegetation has been removed by forest fires or by modern range-management practices such as chaining (removing junipers by means of a huge chain stretched between two bulldozers), chaparral vegetation also is found. Chaparral areas abound in useful plants such as manzanita and mountain mahogany.

Wherever there is water (in the bottoms of canyons with permanent streams or near springs and seeps), the vegetation grows lushly. The canyon bottoms are thick with huge trees such as walnut, alder, cottonwood, and willow that mix along with the conifers of the adjacent forests. Wild grape and many other useful plants are found in the canyon bottoms. In marshy areas there are reeds and cattails, plants that provide fiber and food. Grasshopper Spring is a thriving oasis, with its lovely little waterfall, blooming wild roses, and tangled growth. It was another favorite spot to idle away a Sunday afternoon, although we always had to share the scenery with the cows.

Water, the life-giving necessity of farming people, is surprisingly scarce on this mountain plateau. Cibecue Creek to the east and Canyon Creek to the west were permanent flowing streams, but the plateau itself lacked permanent water. Salt River Draw, the small intermittent stream that once ran through the middle of Grasshopper Pueblo, is the major drainage, but it was an unreliable water source. Today it holds water only after summer thunderstorms. Water for drinking and cooking was most commonly available from springs, seeps, and places where a high water table could be reached with shallow wells. The Mogollon located their pueblos near such springs and seeps; one near Grasshopper Pueblo today is marked by a lush growth of willows and reeds. Such springs in prehistory probably were considered special, even sacred places.

Small kitchen gardens could be watered from seeps and springs, much as the Hopi do today, but snow and rainfall were the primary source of water for crops. Total snow and rainfall average around 20 inches annually in the region. Rain falls primarily in the summer, when masses of moist tropical air from the Gulf of Mexico collide with the hot dry air rising over the mountain ranges in Arizona, producing thunderstorms often accompanied by spectacular lightning displays and destructive hail. The rain falls unevenly across the land. Cloudbursts may flood one area, leaving an adjacent one dry.

Winter rains originating in cyclonic storms in the Pacific Ocean typically are gentler, last longer, and cover a wider area. In the spring and fall there is little rain, and deep snow shrouds the ground in winter.

Most of the year is cool, although the summer temperatures can climb above 100 degrees. In Cibecue, the nearest station with weather records, the hottest month is July, averaging about 92° F. January is the coldest month, with the temperature dropping to a chilly average of 22° F. Although the growing season of 140 days is ample for agriculture, throughout most of prehistory the availability of edible wild plants and the abundance of animals made farming less productive and less reliable than hunting and gathering for the small groups of people who called the mountains home.

The animal life that inhabits the plateau is astonishing in its richness and diversity. Birds are particularly abundant and were useful to the Mogollon. Quail, turkey, and doves were hunted for food, as were transient waterfowl such as geese, ducks, and swans. Eagles and hawks were central to rituals. Today, jays, crows, mockingbirds, and woodpeckers fill the days with their busy racket, and owls large and small add their calls to the sounds of the night. Mice, wood rats, Abert's squirrels with their jaunty tasseled ears, gophers, cottontails, and jackrabbits are seemingly everywhere. The skunk was an all-too-frequent visitor to camp, often taking up residence under cabins and dormitories. Larger but not more dangerous are bobcats, foxes, and the coyotes who sing in the meadows at night. Much bigger *and* potentially dangerous are black bears. Although grizzly bears do not inhabit the area today, these huge bears likely lived near Grasshopper when it was occupied by the Mogollon. Mule deer were more common in prehistoric times; today one is equally likely to encounter the smaller white-tailed deer.

Not all resources were living. The pines and meadows cloak rich outcrops of limestone and sandstone that provided naturally fractured building blocks for the pueblos. Mineral resources were more valuable to prehistoric people than to modern commercial enterprise. A high quality chert for making sharp-edged stone tools erodes out of limestone bedrock along the western edge of the plateau. Farther west, near the Rock House on the Q Ranch Plateau, there is black steatite to make beads and other ornaments. South along the Salt River are the salt banks, and high in the cliffs above there is a turquoise mine. The iron mineral hematite, which provided red paint for decorating pots and many other objects, is abundant along upper Canyon Creek.

We think it unlikely that there were major changes between the environment that the Grasshopper Mogollon knew and the one that was our summer home for so many years. Certainly modern range-management practices have cleared away the juniper and other woodland trees from immense tracts of land, creating brush chaparral where none existed previously. We also think that overexploitation of many plants and animals was likely in prehistoric times. As we will discuss later, the Mogollon simply became too skilled in hunting, drastically reducing what had been a thriving mule deer population. Over time, most of the trees in the vicinity of the pueblo probably were cut for construction wood and for fuel. We also think that farmland became scarce. The growing population tilled all the available land, and decades of continued farming reduced its fertility. Most of these effects were relatively transitory, however, and the plants, animals, and soil returned to their previous conditions after people abandoned the Grasshopper Plateau.

Making a Living at Grasshopper Pueblo

Making a living at Grasshopper Pueblo involved several major components. Unlike their contemporary Hohokam and Anasazi neighbors, who had committed to agriculture many centuries earlier, most of the mountain Mogollon continued to emphasize hunting and gathering until the early 1300s. Mogollon living at Grasshopper Pueblo after 1300 also pursued their traditional hunting and gathering ways as long as they could. Farming became more important as the pueblo grew and constraints on their traditional subsistence practices developed, until the Grasshopper folk had become full-time farmers. And throughout the history of Grasshopper Pueblo, manufacturing and exchange were important economic activities not related directly to obtaining food. We consider these components in turn.

Hunting and Domestic Animals

To the Mogollon, hunting was never a sport or simply a means of getting food. It was a way of structuring life by determining the tempo of movement across the land and establishing social ties and cultural values. It would be consistent for their religion to have emphasized rituals of the hunt and the special powers of animals, but we will never know for certain if this was the case. Because the technology and skills of the hunt were the same as those of combat, no doubt it was the skills of the hunter that ensured protection during periods of unrest.

Zooarchaeologists Stanley and John Olsen have spent years analyzing and cataloging the animal remains from Grasshopper Pueblo. They have

Stephanie Whittlesey uses water flotation to recover plant parts and small animal bones for reconstructing subsistence and diet at Grasshopper Pueblo.

identified a long, diverse list of animals that were hunted, trapped, and caught. We know from the quantities of animal bone and the extraordinary number of arrow points recovered from Grasshopper that wild game was an important part of the diet, particularly early in the pueblo's history. Certain animals were staples, providing a variety of tools and materials as well as food. Rabbits represent nearly 20 percent of the faunal remains analyzed by John Olsen. This numerical abundance is deceiving, because it takes many rabbits to equal the amount of meat provided by a single deer. Nevertheless, rabbits were ubiquitous and commonly hunted. No traces of the technology that was used to capture rabbits have been preserved for us to study. Many Native Americans hunted rabbits by community drives, and huge nets that we think probably were used prehistorically in such drives have been preserved in dry caves on the Colorado Plateau. A similar strategy may have been used at Grasshopper.

Perhaps most important to the people of Grasshopper was the mule deer. Although venison was undoubtedly highly prized, deer provided tools, clothing, and many other things in addition to food. Butchering marks on the bones suggest that deer were quartered in the field before the meat was brought back to camp.

Leon Lorentzen showed in his analysis of stone projectile points that the Grasshopper Spring Anasazi gave up using the atlatl and dart to join the Mogollon in using the bow and arrow. One result of this change in weaponry would have been to increase hunting effectiveness, especially of mule deer. Clearly the Grasshopper people were skilled deer hunters. The widespread adoption of the bow and arrow by skilled hunters combined with a rapidly growing human population to signal the end of dependence on the hunting way of life. The deer were hunted so efficiently that soon there were too few to sustain the people.

There were only two domesticated animals at Grasshopper—dog and turkey. There were two types of dogs, a small dog that was more common and a larger, longer-limbed dog that may have approached collie size. Dogs functioned as a first-alert warning device as well as a sanitation machine, cleaning up scraps, bones, and all sorts of waste from the public areas. They were infrequently skinned and even more rarely eaten.

The domesticated turkeys raised at Grasshopper were larger than their wild cousins. Eggshells and the bones of immature birds or poults were found in rooms bordering Plaza 2, where the turkeys probably were kept penned. About 2 percent of the many turkey bones recovered show cut marks, and these may not all be the result of butchering. Turkeys apparently were kept for their feathers and not just for food. Turkey feathers were prized by the Anasazi for making warm blankets and for decorating prayer sticks and other objects. In their homeland on the Colorado Plateau, the Anasazi reared domestic turkeys in such numbers that they created a sort of cottage industry. Archaeologist Erik Reed, who wrote a number of articles describing the contrasts between the Mogollon and the Anasazi, once noted that the Mogollon did not eat turkeys or keep them for their feathers. We think that the Grasshopper people learned about the value of keeping turkeys from the Anasazi who lived with them at Grasshopper Pueblo, and, indeed, it may have been the Anasazi themselves who were the turkey raisers.

Wild Plant Gathering

It is difficult to say for certain, but it is probably true that in the early days of hunting, gathering, and gardening it was the gathering of wild plant foods by women that contributed most of the calories in the diet. Grasshopper is in an ideal location to benefit from the plant foods of the desert and the mountains, as the Western Apache knew. Women could travel to the lower elevations to gather the fruits and buds of many types of cactus, yucca, and perhaps also the bean pods of the mesquite tree. Intermediate elevations, depending on the nearness of water, provided acorns, walnuts, and mescal, and higher up in the mountains, piñon nuts and juniper berries were collected.

A catalog of plants recovered at Grasshopper indicates the breadth and diversity of the species that were used as food, medicine, and dye. Paleobotanist Vorsila Bohrer found that some of the most important plants were manzanita and juniper, to judge by their frequency of occurrence. The berries could be dried and formed into a cake. Manzanita berries also make a tart, refreshing drink. Cactus was a food that could be prepared many different ways. The fruit could be eaten fresh, boiled to make syrup or a beverage, or dried. Cactus seeds could be made into a cake that stored well. Tender cactus buds, the first fresh food of spring, were roasted. The seeds of many grasses and annual plants such as tansy mustard, sunflower, and amaranth were parched, ground into meal, and then made into a gruel or formed into cakes. No doubt the greens of some of these plants also were boiled and eaten as a sort of wild spinach. Other important plants were yucca, bear grass, wild grape, walnut, piñon, cattail, and squawbush. Many of these plants also served medicinal uses, and others provided dye for baskets and cloth. Some were used in making basketry, matting, and twine and in the construction of houses.

The Cibecue Apache say that the piñon nuts around Grasshopper are not very good, but the mescal is among the best on the reservation. We are unsure about the importance of mescal in the Mogollon diet. Archaeologists have long believed that the presence of agave plants at archaeological sites signals its use prehistorically, as the plants grow easily from seeds and plant parts discarded in the trash. Agave grows today at Grasshopper and Chodistaas Pueblos, suggesting that the plant was introduced by the people living there. No agave remains have been found at Grasshopper Pueblo, however, and none were recovered from Canyon Creek Pueblo, except the spines that were used as needles. Another traditional indicator of mescal processing is the presence of so-called agave knives. These tabular stone knives are thought to have been used to harvest the plants. We have recovered such knives from Grasshopper.

Regardless of the extent to which the wild agave plants were used, the Grasshopper Mogollon probably gathered them much like the Apache did.

The plants were trimmed down to the tender hearts, the sharp, spiny leaves were removed, and the hearts were roasted in pits. The end product was a highly nutritious, compact, and storable food. The stalk, soon after it appears, is very sweet and was eaten like sugarcane.

Farming

Farming was a relatively risky enterprise. Arable soil that was deep enough to plant was limited around Grasshopper Pueblo, and erosion was a constant problem. The Mogollon were certainly aware that some soils were better than others, to judge by the close correlation between archaeological sites and good agricultural soils. The best soils in the mountains are to the south, along Oak Creek.

The Grasshopper farmers located their agricultural fields on the floodplains of the creeks, where crops could absorb ground moisture, and on higher ground to collect slope runoff. The farming technology was simple, consisting only of erosion control and soil conservation features. We have found such simple stone features throughout the area. Check dams set across small drainages slowed the rush of water onto a field and directed its flow outward. Linear borders paralleled the contours of gentle slopes to collect and retain soil. We have been unable to identify any irrigation ditches on the Grasshopper Plateau similar to those used historically by the Cibecue Apache, but this does not necessarily mean that none were used. We think it more likely that when agricultural shortfalls became chronic, the Grasshopper people chose to establish new settlements for bringing additional land under cultivation, rather than convert to a new technology such as irrigation. Moreover, there are no rivers or creeks on the Grasshopper Plateau to provide irrigation water.

Cultivation was carried out without benefit of metal tools, using stone hoes and simple wooden digging sticks. We cannot say who did the planting, weeding, and harvesting. Among the Hopi, the men are the farmers, although everyone helps with the harvest. We imagine that the children were regularly stationed in the fields to keep the pesky crows, squirrels, and rabbits away from the growing crops.

Despite this simple farming technology, the Mogollon grew four major crops quite successfully. These were corn, common beans (*Phaseolus vulgaris*), squash, and cotton. Literally tons of grinding stones have been recovered from habitation rooms at Grasshopper Pueblo, attesting to the importance of corn and suggesting how it was prepared. Corn was most typically ground into meal on a large slab metate, fashioned from sandstone or quartzite. We think that cornmeal was mixed with water and boiled as gruel or formed into cakes and baked. Fresh corn could be roasted, which no doubt was a treat. There is no evidence that the people prepared tortillas or the wafer-thin, papery bread that the Hopi call *piki,* both of which require a thin, flat baking stone or griddle. Beans probably were boiled, although it takes a great deal of time to cook beans to an edible stage in a pot over a wood fire. Squash most likely was dried and then stewed.

Although we tend to think of cotton as a crop of warmer climates, the varieties grown by the Anasazi and by the Hopi in modern times were adapted to higher, colder elevations such as Grasshopper. The seeds we recovered certainly suggest that cotton was grown near the pueblo. Raw cotton was abundant at Canyon Creek Pueblo, and charred cotton seeds occur commonly at other Mogollon pueblos, such as Point of Pines. Although the fibers probably were the most important part of the cotton plant, the oil-rich seeds also could be eaten.

Manufacturing and Exchange

It is the rare archaeologist who has never been asked, "Are you looking for gold?" Our answer has always been, "Of course, we're always looking for it, but the archaeologist's gold is not what you think. Gold will never be found in the prehistoric ruins of the American Southwest." Many people find it hard to believe this true answer, that there was no gold, silver, or precious stones such as diamonds and emeralds among the ancient peoples of the Southwest. From Coronado's time onward, legends of gold have led many an adventurer on a vain quest for these stones and metals. The most precious commodities of southwestern prehistory were turquoise, macaws, copper bells, seashells, and cotton and the textiles woven from it.

Archaeologists have devoted considerable attention over the past several decades to investigating prehistoric trade networks in the Southwest. Some have proposed large-scale managed trading systems as the principal explanation for the widespread distribution of certain artifacts that are so apparent in the archaeological record. Complicated economic models have been constructed to account for the movement of valuable commodities and their use in sustaining a managerial elite at the top of the social hierarchy. The evidence from Grasshopper Pueblo suggests that if such a complicated system existed prehistorically in the Southwest, the Grasshopper folk did not participate in it. Let us look first at evidence for manufacturing high-priced

Fourmile Polychrome bowls, thought to be a major item of exchange between Grasshopper Pueblo and settlements on the Colorado Plateau.

goods at Grasshopper Pueblo and then at the evidence for trade and exchange within the region and with distant lands.

Richard Ciolek-Torrello's analysis of room function revealed that a large amount of space at Grasshopper Pueblo was devoted to manufacturing and that most of the manufacturing was oriented toward household and ceremonial items, with only limited manufacturing of export items. Room 113, analyzed by Daniela Triadan, is a good example of manufacturing activities in a household context. The room was devoted to the fabrication of a wide range of domestic items as well as turquoise pendants. On the floor and stored within stone-lined bins were pigments and clay for making pottery. Evidence for the production of flaked stone tools littered the floor in the form of bone flaking implements, unfinished tools and blanks, and abundant flaking debris.

Room 113 also contained turquoise—certainly one of the most valuable commodities of late prehistory—in all stages of manufacture. There were raw nuggets, unfinished pendant blanks, and drilled, finished pendants. Chemical analysis of the turquoise by John Welch and Daniela Triadan confirmed

The skeleton of a macaw brought into Grasshopper Pueblo from present-day Mexico, probably from Casas Grandes in Chihuahua.

that it came from the prehistoric turquoise mine recorded by Emil Haury at the southern edge of the Grasshopper Plateau. What is so intriguing about this turquoise mine is that it appears not to have been guarded, and access to it was not restricted in any noticeable way. We think this absence of any control over access to the turquoise source goes against what would be expected of a complicated, managed trading system in valuable goods. In the Grasshopper turquoise we have evidence for use of a valuable resource in a manufacturing process but no evidence for restricted access to or control of this resource.

Although the only strong evidence for manufacturing items for potential export involves turquoise, it is possible that individuals took advantage of other local resources, such as ceramics, salt, hematite, and high quality chert. It is probable that the long-term joint use of the mountains with unrestricted access to resources continued throughout the period of Grasshopper's occupation.

There is clear evidence that some goods were imported over a considerable distance. Perhaps the most important of these are macaws. These tropical birds were prized for their brightly colored feathers and were never used as food. They were ceremonially buried in the kivas and the Great Kiva, as we will discuss in chapter 6. The macaws found at Grasshopper may have come from Casas Grandes, 300 miles away in the present-day northern Mexican state of Chihuahua. There is no good evidence that macaws were raised at Grasshopper Pueblo. Most of the birds we have recovered are mature and likely were brought into the pueblo as adults. Although some immature birds have been found, the specialized requirements of breeding macaws make it more likely that they were brought into Grasshopper through trade.

There is ample evidence that macaws were bred and raised at Casas Grandes, including the presence of breeding pens and many immature birds.

If the twenty or so macaws found at Grasshopper represent a 20 percent sample, then approximately one hundred macaws found their way into the community. Speculating further, if the height of Grasshopper's occupation lasted fifty years, then about two macaws were obtained each year. This low figure, less than what we would expect of a complicated trade network, indicates a fairly simple kind of exchange.

Copper bells also probably came from Casas Grandes. We have noted that there was no mining, smelting, or metal working in the American Southwest north of the international border. The people of Casas Grandes, evidently related to more technologically sophisticated Mesoamerican peoples, did understand and employ these arts. Copper bells no doubt were used in ornamental and ceremonial contexts.

Many different types of marine shell ornaments were found at Grasshopper. The shells primarily represent mollusks that occur in the Gulf of California (Sea of Cortez), including species of *Glycymeris, Laevicardium, Conus,* and *Turitella*; there are only a few specimens made from Pacific Coast mollusks such as abalone. Only finished shell ornaments have been found and no debris, confirming that shell manufacturing did not take place at Grasshopper. The exchange relationships that had operated throughout much of late prehistory to provide marine shell ornaments to people living a long way from the ocean evidently continued. We suspect that shell, like some of the nonlocally made ceramics, came to Grasshopper in a number of different ways, including simple bartering between individuals at ceremonials and fairs, as well as in the baggage of people on the move looking for a better place to live.

Another important item to the ancient peoples of the Southwest was cotton. Woven cotton textiles were essential as clothing and blankets, and raw cotton and cotton textiles may have figured prominently in ceremonial contexts, if we borrow analogies from modern Native American peoples. At Hopi, for example, elaborate wedding garments and sashes are essential items for the wedding ceremony and are woven specifically for this purpose. Cotton also serves an important ritual function, symbolizing rain clouds. We are only beginning to understand the role of cotton in prehistoric exchange systems, but we know that it was traded widely and that people with productive lands and sufficient water beyond their own needs may have used this excess land to grow cotton for trade. We think it unlikely that this took place at Grasshopper, however.

It is not unexpected that families without land and moving from place to place in search of a new home might well earn a meager and temporary living exchanging exotic, valuable, and even mundane items. We know from the work of ethnographers and ethnoarchaeologists that people without farmland will turn temporarily to the manufacture or exchange of craft items to earn a living until they acquire land of their own.

Tools of Everyday Life

When Reid started teaching the anthropology class "Prehistoric Peoples of the Southwest" at the University of Arizona, he thought it was a great idea to have students make a tool or other object that was common in prehistoric times in the Southwest—an arrow point, basket, or some such thing—using only tools and materials available to ancient peoples. He wanted today's urban students to acquire an appreciation for how difficult it is to gather materials and make everything needed to survive with a so-called primitive technology. Then, when students compared what they had crafted to actual prehistoric artifacts displayed in the museum, they would further appreciate the skill and experience of ancient artisans. Reid quickly realized that, in addition to representing an exercise in futility and frustration, the class project threatened to strip bare much of the campus vegetation and to redistribute decorative stone. One favorite project was a hafted "ax," made from an unmodified river rock collected from one of the desert landscaping areas, with an extremely green tree branch bent around it and tied with ordinary string—obviously something fashioned that morning before class. A few students got the message that the project was meant to convey, but the price to campus ecology was too heavy for it to continue, and he was forced to seek out other ways to convey the simple truths of ancient life.

An appreciation of the difficult task the students faced requires just a little imagination. Picture camping outdoors without all of the useful and necessary items furnished by sporting goods, grocery, and hardware stores—tent, metal tools, matches, down sleeping bags, camp stove, flashlight, freeze-dried food, bottled water, propane lantern—and lacking transportation other than one's own legs and means of communication other than the human voice. What if everything that you wore, used, or ate was fashioned by your own or someone else's hands? Imagine further coping with an unexpected thunderstorm or snowstorm, an accident, or childbirth under these conditions. This would come close to what everyday life at Grasshopper Pueblo was like.

Every item that was used by the people of Grasshopper had to be fashioned by hand from available materials, usually stone, bone, or wood. The knowledge necessary to acquire the materials, fashion the tool, and eventually use it had to be passed down verbally from one person to another. There were no instruction manuals. Even a simple meal required what is to modern city dwellers unimaginable effort. Every food item was grown, hunted, or collected, not purchased at the corner grocery store, and each was prepared without the luxuries of the modern kitchen. The meat for the stew was killed and butchered with stone tools made by hand. The corn was ground with stone mano and metate, also laboriously fashioned using other stone tools. The stew was cooked in a pot made by hand, with water fetched from a spring in a jar also made by hand, over a fire for which someone had to collect wood and light without benefit of matches or flint and steel. The clay for the cooking pots and serving bowls had to be found, collected, and processed before the pots could be made and fired; the stone for the tools had to be found, tested, and fashioned into arrow points, knives, and metates. The kitchen itself was built with stone carried considerable distances and beams cut with polished stone axes, tools that someone had to first make. And our recitation does not consider failures—the pot that cracks in firing, the stone too poor to flake, the deer that got away. It is exhausting simply to contemplate this effort.

Even in ancient times, when craft skills and dexterity were widespread, some people were better at certain tasks than others. We imagine that some women in the pueblo were more skilled potters, even though most women made pottery. Some were better basket makers, and others made finer cotton sashes and shirts. Despite the opportunistic nature of hunting, some men always brought back more game. Such differential distribution of skills made it possible for individuals and individual households to swap skills, raw materials, and finished products within the community and thus avoid having to make everything from scratch. This exchange in basic goods and services also performed the important social function of binding households together in a network of obligation and dependence. Ethnographic information tells us that households without land or needing to supplement poor crop yields will temporarily turn to making items to barter for food. But regardless of all the many ways villagers may acquire raw materials and finished equipment, every household had to know how to survive on its own knowledge and skills alone. An enormous amount of time each day was devoted to the tasks of making, repairing, and maintaining tools and equipment. The most basic were tools for hunting, pots for cooking and storage, grinding stones for preparing corn and other plant foods, and basketry and textiles for multiple purposes.

Tools of the Hunt

John Whittaker's research comparing flaked stone arrow points made by contemporary flintknappers to the Grasshopper arrow points documents the fact that these delicate chert tools were skillfully made by individual hunters rather than craft specialists. The hundreds of arrow points recovered from Grasshopper, along with the impressive quantity of animal bone, clearly indicate the importance of hunting. But it was not until Leon Lorentzen brought his experience as a hunter to the field school research team that we really began to understand the vital role of hunting at Grasshopper Pueblo.

In his master's thesis, Lorentzen defined how the Grasshopper Mogollon made arrows. Working with the local chert, he was able to duplicate the typical triangular arrow points, some with notches on each side that would be fastened to a hardwood foreshaft with deer sinew. The foreshaft would then be attached to a cane mainshaft that had been smoothed and trued with a heated arrowshaft straightener made of steatite. Feathers, most probably from birds of a particular type or color that identified the hunter or reflected his family or ritual memberships, would give the missile stability in flight. No bows have been found at Grasshopper, but the ones examined by Lorentzen from similar contexts have a simple curve and a pull in the range of 30 to 50 pounds.

The stone-tipped cane arrow would not have had the penetrating power of an atlatl-thrown spear, yet it was vastly superior in other attributes. One advantage was in the rapid reloading capacity of the bow and arrow, a semi-automatic weapon compared to the atlatl or spear thrower. Another was in the flatter trajectory and greater speed at which the lighter arrow could travel. These qualities made the bow and arrow a far more versatile weapon for hunting and defense than the atlatl and dart. Little wonder, then, that the Grasshopper Spring Anasazi appeared to have quickly given up the atlatl in favor of the bow and arrow toward the end of the upheaval caused by the Great Drought.

A tool kit for making arrows

The bow and arrow would have increased the deadliness of the hunter, particularly in bringing down deer. Deer provided the Grasshopper Mogollon with a wide array of raw materials for tools and artifacts as well as food. Buckskins could be tanned for clothing, footgear, containers, or anything made with leather and could be traded with farming people less skilled in the hunt, as did the Western Apache much later. Deer provided sinew essential for sewing hides and making tools and many other items. Antlers were used for hammers and flaking tools. Leg bones had many uses. From them were made awls to create basketry and sew hides, beamers to clean hair from hides, and raw material to fashion ornamental rings. Men wore highly polished hairpins made from leg bones. Tinklers to decorate clothing, quivers, and other objects were made from deer hoofs, and the lower jaws provided ceremonial rasps. The mule deer was a mainstay of the Mogollon diet and a storehouse of raw materials essential to mountain life. When overhunting, along with other factors, contributed to a reduction in deer numbers later in the occupation of Grasshopper Pueblo, it created a critical nutritional and economic shortfall.

Pottery for Household Cooking and Storage

The American Southwest, today as well as in ancient times, is world renowned for the technological sophistication and the aesthetic beauty of its
Native American pottery. The Grasshopper Mogollon, however, much like
the Western Apache, did not contribute significantly to this aesthetic tradition. Except for the intricate geometric designs and simple life-form representations of the Mimbres Mogollon, most of the Mogollon throughout their
long history placed more importance on baskets and other woven containers
than pottery for a wide variety of everyday tasks and especially as a background for decoration.

During the several centuries preceding aggregation at Grasshopper Pueblo,
the mountain Mogollon had perfected the making of corrugated pots in a
variety of patterns that mimicked the bold designs on their baskets. Painting
these designs with white was the height of most Mogollon pottery decoration
until the Anasazi arrived. The Mogollon would learn techniques of pottery
decoration from the resident Anasazi, as well as better ways to farm corn. We
will discuss the painted pottery that they learned to make in chapter 6.

Corrugated pots were used for cooking and storage. These textured,
rough-surfaced pots belie the skill and effort required in their manufacture.
Women, whom we assume were the ones who made the pots with no evidence to the contrary, collected clays from deposits near Grasshopper that
fire to a brown color. Crushed rock was used as temper, which helps to bind
the clay together and keeps the pot from cracking when drying. Clay and
temper were crushed and ground on the metate, and the clay was sifted.
Mixed with water, the materials were kneaded together like bread dough.

The Mogollon made their pottery by a technique we call coil and scrape.
Thin ropes of clay are rolled between the palms and then coiled up in a
circular fashion to build the walls of the vessel, which resemble corrugated
cardboard or clapboard house siding. The coils are then pinched together on
the exterior and smoothed by light scraping and wiping, which obliterates
the corrugations. The interior is scraped completely smooth, so food won't
stick and stew can be stirred. After air drying for some time, the pots were
fired in an open fire, producing brown or grayish pottery with darker fire
clouds. There is no evidence that the Mogollon used simple kilns to fire their
pottery, although the Anasazi did use such facilities.

The process is deceptively simple sounding, as anyone who has tried to
make pottery using these traditional methods and materials will know. It
requires knowledge to locate the right kind of clay and add just the right

Everyday utility pottery for cooking and eating

amount of temper. Add too much, and the product is like sand; add too little, and the pot will crack or even fall apart. Coiling takes patience and skill to form a symmetrical, circular vessel, pinching and scraping hurt the fingers, and the entire process takes time. Firing is probably the most critical aspect, for if the pot is still wet or if there is a piece of foreign material like limestone trapped in the clay, it will crack or even explode. Because of the tricky, even whimsical nature of the process, modern Native American potters ensure their pot making will succeed with many small prayers and charms, and no doubt this was true of the Grasshopper potters as well.

One can appreciate the skill of the Grasshopper potters even more when understanding the size and variety of the household pottery assemblage. Jars, bowls, and plates were needed in various sizes and shapes, and each household used several of each category. Medium-sized jars with a capacity of a gallon or two were used for cooking. We envision stew, made with the gathered foods of the day, corn and other vegetables, and occasionally meat, simmering all day long over a slow fire, enriched occasionally when a new item was tossed into the bubbling mixture. Stew pots used in this way display a great deal of smoke blackening and sooting. This method of cooking helps to wring as much nutritional value from corn as possible and is about the only way that beans can be made edible.

Large jars, reaching a capacity of 25 gallons, were used for storage of grains and foodstuffs susceptible to invasion by insects, rodents, or fungus. Pottery provides virtually pest-free and moisture-proof storage. Similar large pots no doubt were used as water storage containers. The tops of storage jars were sealed with a plug of clay, basketry, or leather or a flat sandstone disk. At Canyon Creek Pueblo, Haury recovered a storage jar with a capacity of 60 gallons (7.5 bushels) that could only have been placed in the room before the room was finished—the pot is too large to fit through the doorway.

Bowls were used as serving vessels and individual eating dishes and in a variety of everyday tasks. A bowl was kept in the mealing bin to hold the meal as it was ground on the metate. Decorated bowls served as containers for a variety of nondomestic tasks as well and were typical burial accompaniments.

The quantities of broken pottery—literally millions of potsherds—recovered from Grasshopper Pueblo attest to the number of vessels in use and their rate of breakage. Although we suspect that most of the pueblo's women made pots, they must have spent a great deal of their time producing and replacing the household's primary container.

Not until the Grasshopper Mogollon had been convinced of their future as settled village farmers did they begin to see pottery as a medium for decoration as well as a practical container for storing corn and for making venison stew. It is this property of prehistoric pottery to reflect a broad range of practical, social, and symbolic characteristics of human existence that makes it the single most informative artifact for understanding the prehistory of Grasshopper Pueblo.

Grinding Stones

Perhaps the most significant and necessary pieces of equipment for the Mogollon household were grinding tools. A multitude of tasks required mano and metate, from processing cactus fruits and other wild plant foods, to pulverizing clay and pigments for pottery making, to producing flour or meal from dried corn, sedge and cattail pollen, and parched seeds. Every household had several metates, which are the large bottom or nether stone, and manos—Spanish for "hand"—of different sizes and shapes. Household grinding equipment probably was almost always in use for one purpose or another; simply grinding enough corn for each day's meals was a time-consuming task.

Making a shaped metate is not an easy matter. Large cobbles of the right material with the appropriate texture must be located. Although basalt was favored for metates by the Hohokam and other desert peoples, the Mogollon used locally available quartzite and dense sandstone. Large flakes were hammered off the stone to shape it roughly at the quarry site. The roughly shaped stone was carried home, where the final shaping was completed. Needless to say, the process requires considerable energy and time. For this reason, the Mogollon likely collected metates from earlier, abandoned settlements and recycled them, just as the Western Apache did hundreds of years later. Worn metates could be reshaped for other uses.

Basketry, Weaving, and Textiles

As one might expect of a mobile people who spent much time in the hunt and in wild plant gathering, containers and objects of perishable materials were extremely important to the Mogollon. What we know of basketry and weaving at Grasshopper Pueblo comes by analogy from Canyon Creek Pueblo, for few woven materials survived the open, unprotected conditions of Grasshopper Pueblo. When excavating at Canyon Creek Pueblo, Emil Haury found evidence for several types of basketry, although almost all were made from bear grass. Storage granaries, which were set into the room floors, were made of crude, coiled basketry and were covered with clay. Baskets of different construction served many uses. Coarse-coiled baskets made of bear grass and silvertop bluestem grass were used to cover the granaries and for storage. Close-coiled baskets were more finely woven and were used for numerous purposes. There also were wickerwork and twilled baskets.

Matting made of bear grass or reeds was used to cover floors, as backing for cradles, and as sleeping mats. Cordage was made from yucca, cotton, and a fibrous plant called apocynum. Bags, clothing, and many other items were made of cordage. Haury recovered agave-spine needles with bits of cordage still attached.

The Mogollon were skilled spinners, weavers, and dyers. Cotton and apocynum were used to make textiles. Both fibers were spun by hand, using a wooden spindle and a spindle whorl to weight the shaft. The flat, disk-shaped spindle whorls were made from drilled potsherds or wood. Natural dyes are abundant and include plant materials such as walnut hulls, sunflower seeds, the root of algerita bushes, and willow bark. Most natural dyes

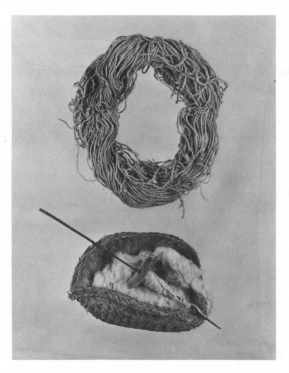

Fibers from Canyon Creek Pueblo: a skein of apocynum yarn (top), and a basket of raw cotton containing a wooden spindle partially filled with spun yarn.

yield yellow, green, and brown colors. Minerals may have been used to achieve darker hues. Simple floor looms were probably used to weave the fiber into cloth that was used in blankets, garments, sashes, and bags.

Canyon Creek produced abundant evidence for spinning and weaving cotton fabrics. Haury recovered a woven basket that contained raw cotton fibers and a spindle that was partially filled with spun yarn. This spinning kit was buried with a woman who was wrapped in a plain, woven cotton blanket finished with tassels. Another burial was wrapped in a tie-dyed cotton blanket. Most cotton blankets were a fine plain weave, generally a natural color, although brown, yellow, and white yarns also were used. A decorative effect could be achieved on plain weaves by wrapping the weft yarns around the warp. Haury also recovered a fragment of compound cloth with a geometric design in brown and white.

Apocynum fibers are coarser than cotton and produced textiles resembling modern burlap or gunny sacking. There also were combined cotton and apocynum textiles. Apocynum cloth is naturally brown, and the only dyed example found at Canyon Creek Pueblo was black. At Canyon Creek apocynum textiles were used only as wrappings for the dead.

Becoming Farmers

We have seen that the people of Chodistaas Pueblo relied on hunting, wild plant gathering, and gardening of corn and beans, a mixed strategy well suited to a mobile people who moved seasonally between the mountains and adjacent desert lowlands and north on to the Colorado Plateau. After 1300, people living at Grasshopper Pueblo pursued their traditional hunting and gathering ways as long as they could. John Welch and David Tuggle, each approaching the problem from different viewpoints in dissertation research, independently concluded that the Grasshopper Mogollon accomplished the transition from hunting, gathering, and gardening to being village farmers totally dependent on corn agriculture in a little more than a generation. We think that it was the Anasazi living in the mountains who served as a catalyst for the rapid transition to food production at Grasshopper.

Environmental deterioration over the years of the Great Drought created agricultural shortages throughout the Colorado Plateau, forcing the Western Anasazi, or Hisatsinom—the master dry farmers of the Southwest—to move into the central mountains. There were three important consequences of Anasazi settlement of the mountains that affected this transition.

First, the presence of Anasazi people restricted the seasonal movement and access to wild food resources that the Grasshopper Mogollon had long enjoyed. An inconvenient characteristic of wild plant foods is that they are only available at certain times and in certain places. Where once it was possible for a Mogollon household to move from place to place according to nature's seasonal schedule, the increase in population restricted traditional patterns of mobility. It became necessary to send out gathering parties farther away from home to collect the plant foods and bring them back to Grasshopper for processing. Wild plant foods became more and more expensive because of the time and energy it took to collect them. In addition, wild plant foods are replenished at nature's pace, which in time proved much too slow for them to continue to be a reliable food source for a rapidly growing population. The Grasshopper Mogollon were about to learn a fact of life known to their Anasazi and Hohokam neighbors for centuries.

The Mogollon began to stay longer and longer at places that once were occupied only seasonally. At the same time, the newcomers competed with the Mogollon and among themselves for necessary resources, creating a threatening situation. Small communities were vulnerable to raiders seeking food and captives. The second consequence of Anasazi occupation of the mountains was aggregation, as people abandoned their small villages and banded together with others from similar villages at Grasshopper.

Third, the Anasazi transmitted their knowledge of arid land farming techniques to the Mogollon who lived with them at Grasshopper. As we have seen, the Mogollon were traditionally rather desultory and small-scale farmers who vastly preferred to live by hunting and gathering when it was feasible to do so. The Anasazi, by contrast, had a long history of intensive and successful farming on the high, arid Colorado Plateau.

The population explosion at Grasshopper Pueblo happened during a time of unusually high snow and rainfall, which created ideal conditions for farming. At the same time, the Anasazi living in the Grasshopper region, having perfected dry-farming techniques on the Colorado Plateau, adapted their traditional corn agriculture to the mountains. They were uniquely suited to share their unsurpassed farming knowledge and skills with the Mogollon. For an undetermined period in the early 1300s, the traditional Mogollon hunting-gathering-gardening subsistence strategy existed side by side with the Anasazi emphasis on dry farming. In time, as the Grasshopper population increased and the animals and wild plants decreased in abundance, the Mogollon were forced to learn how to be successful dry farmers, and they quickly came to depend on agriculture as their way of life.

The Grasshopper case illustrates two important points in the adoption of food production. First, the shift to complete dependence on agriculture was not the product of any single cause. It was created by the interaction of numerous variables, including climatic change, technological change, competition for scarce resources, residential stability, and population size, density, and movement. Second, it illustrates that knowledge of food production is necessary but insufficient alone for change to take place. The Mogollon had knowledge of farming and had practiced gardening for centuries, sometimes alongside the Anasazi, but they committed wholeheartedly to agriculture only when wild resources had been depleted through population increase and overexploitation of wild plants and animals. Once they made the change they stuck to it, preferring to leave the mountains to pursue an agricultural way of life in other areas where this life-style was possible over the long term.

Consequences of Dependence on Agriculture

We often think of agriculture as easing the burdens of everyday life in ancient times. It provides a food supply that is relatively stable and more predictable than wild foods such as piñon, which may offer a bumper crop one year and then fail entirely for the next two years. Yet the success of an agricultural life-style in terms of health and longevity depends on the plants that are cultivated. Surprisingly, corn is not a highly nutritious food. It supplies carbohydrates, fiber, and calories but is deficient in protein, important minerals, and amino acids. Corn contains little iron or calcium, minerals needed for strong bones and healthy blood cells, and is deficient in niacin. Corn also contains substances that can deplete the human body of nutrients. The hulls of corn kernels contain phytate, which inhibits the intestinal absorption of iron and calcium. Phytate also binds what little calcium is present in maize as well as calcium from other foods. Corn also contains a toxic constituent that reduces the activity of enzymes that break down proteins. A diet high in corn can produce anemia, rickets, and other serious diseases.

These effects can be reduced or eliminated by using high heat to prepare corn and by soaking corn with alkali or lime before cooking. Lime pretreatment removes the phytate-containing hulls of the corn kernels. Grinding corn with mano and metate can add significant amounts of iron and calcium from the included grit, depending on the stone used to make the metate. There is no way to know if the Grasshopper Mogollon practiced lime pretreatment, but the biological data suggest that they did not.

The consequences of what must have been a diet largely devoted to corn are seen in the biological remains of the people who died and were buried at Grasshopper Pueblo. Biological anthropologist Madeleine Hinkes examined the bones of children and found widespread abnormalities indicating food shortage and anemia during the growth years. She found evidence that the sources of this nutritional stress were chronic as well as acute, indicating that the overall poor nutrition was punctuated by episodes of extreme food shortage.

The incidence of dental pathology was extraordinarily high among the Grasshopper people, including caries, abscessed teeth, and tooth loss. Many teeth also showed evidence that enamel development was interrupted, indicating infectious disease or malnutrition. Even otherwise healthy teeth exhibited tremendous wear caused by eating foods replete with bits of stone from the metates and manos used to grind corn. We can relate the extreme dental pathology to the diet. Soft, sticky, high carbohydrate foods such as cornmeal cakes and gruel provided the perfect environment for the growth of oral bacteria and plaque and also contained lots of tooth-wearing grit. The caries-causing, iron-poor corn diet, coupled with low protein intake and lack of systematic oral hygiene, was disastrous to tooth health.

Perhaps also indicative of poor nutrition and associated physical stress was the extraordinary infant mortality rate. A striking 56 percent of the recovered burials—a figure unusual even for preindustrial societies lacking modern medical care—are children under the age of twelve. No doubt simple illnesses that today are little cause for alarm, such as respiratory and intestinal ailments, claimed the lives of many babies. An unweaned infant dependent on mother's milk would be affected by her diet, as well. If the diet was poor, the baby would suffer accordingly.

Western Apache and Hopi Models for Grasshopper Subsistence

Alternate ways of earning a living at Grasshopper were never numerous, and as time went on and as the number of people increased, the opportunities available to any household lessened. As natural resources dwindled, people were forced either into full-time farming or moving away to pursue their traditional way of life elsewhere. Some may have turned to crafts such as pottery making as a temporary means of earning a living; others may have peddled shell or turquoise ornaments throughout the plateau and farther afield in hopes of making a reasonable living.

Although we will never know the economic decisions made by individuals, several general features of Grasshopper ecology are clear. The household was the basic economic and social group within which the decisions for adapting and surviving were made, and it fell to individual members of the household to excel at traditional tasks and to learn new ones as necessary. The contrast between Mogollon and Anasazi lifeways tells us that not all prehistoric farmers in the Southwest were alike. For Mogollon households, hunting and gathering rather quickly gave way to a farming way of life and, ultimately, after a brief return to seasonal mobility, to moving out of their mountain homeland, never to live there again. Anasazi households, on the other hand, after several generations in the mountains where they farmed, made pottery, and taught others these skills, resumed their traditional adaptation as settled villagers and master dry farmers of the Southwest's most inhospitable plateau environments.

The contrast is illuminated by comparing these life-styles with those of two modern Native American peoples, the Western Apache and the Hopi. The Western Apache, who lived in the Arizona mountains from sometime in the 1600s until they were forced onto the reservations in the nineteenth century, maintained a life-style that was markedly similar to that of the Mogollon, at least until the 1300s. Grenville Goodwin, an anthropologist who lived with and studied the Western Apache in the early twentieth century, gave us a detailed picture of what prereservation Western Apache life was like. Goodwin estimated that wild plant and animal foods each made up between 35 and 40 percent of the Apache diet, and farm products contributed the remainder. The scheduling of activities was determined primarily by seasonal availability and abundance of wild foods. Most of their time was occupied in collecting wild plant foods. Hunting, although concentrated in the early spring and fall, took place throughout the year. Farming received little attention except during planting and harvesting. According to Winfred Buskirk, another ethnographer who studied the Western Apache, "the amount of wild plant foods utilized fluctuated with the abundance of the agricultural harvests and with the success of hunting and raiding expeditions."

Mescal, the most important wild food plant to the Apache, appears to have played a minor role in the Grasshopper diet for reasons we do not fully understand. The other wild plant foods of the mountain region and adjacent areas—acorns, piñon nuts, walnuts, seeds and greens of herbaceous plants, juniper berries, sunflower seeds, mesquite beans, cactus fruits, and yucca—were a mainstay for the Apache and the Mogollon alike.

The area needed to feed an Apache family was large, and it was necessary for people to move from camp to camp throughout the year. After planting their fields in May, the Apache moved south to the Salt River to collect cactus fruits during June and July. The people moved among gathering areas to collect acorns, mesquite, and yucca during the late summer and early fall before returning to mountain farms to harvest crops and collect piñon nuts and juniper berries. Throughout the winter the Apache gathered wild plants and hunted. Recent research by John Welch confirms that our use of an Apache model for the Mogollon living in the Grasshopper region prior to the Aggregation period is appropriate.

This analogy between the lifeways of the Grasshopper Mogollon and the Western Apache is no longer accurate, however, for the time following the early 1300s. Then, the Mogollon were rapidly forced by circumstances to shift their subsistence away from wild plants and animals to farming. Although their rapidly growing dependence upon corn for sustenance is clearly evident in Grasshopper's archaeological record, corn was never as thoroughly integrated into their language, symbol, myth, and life as it was with the historical Hopi.

To the Hopi, corn is the metaphor of life. Its life cycle is seen as the symbol of human growth. "People are corn," "Corn is our mother," and "Young corn plants are maidens," say the Hopi. All Hopi ceremonies, according to ethnographer Maitland Bradfield, are focused on bringing rain, fertility, and growth of crops. This philosophical union of the ideological and ecological domains of daily life focused on corn was not achieved by the Grasshopper Mogollon.

The bits and pieces of the archaeological record that bear on this question point to the inescapable conclusion that Grasshopper ideology was in a state of transition between a hunter-gatherer's freedom to move like the wind and a farmer's commitment to land, labor, and community cooperation. For example, no Hopi man, it is said, will marry a girl unless she can make piki. We have never found a piki stone, or even a fragment of one, at Grasshopper Pueblo or at any of the other communities in the region.

Whereas there may have been less pressure to revise their ideology as they became farmers, the demands of daily life required that the Grasshopper Mogollon rather quickly adjust the rules and relationships required to live in a crowded pueblo community. We turn to these social relationships next in chapter 5.

5

Grasshopper Sociology

The Grasshopper research program of the 1960s broke new ground in attempting to investigate social phenomena through the archaeological record. Convinced that archaeology was anthropology or it was nothing, archaeologists sought to reconstruct kinship systems, rules of residence and descent, and other social relationships. This is an extremely difficult task with archaeological data, however, and we no longer view many of the ground-breaking studies of the 1960s as valid reconstructions of the past. Today, archaeologists do not seek to reconstruct rules of descent or residence after marriage, preferring instead to identify those relationships and groups that can be inferred from the archaeological record with confidence. Nevertheless, these early studies of social organization did serve an important function. They alerted us to the possibilities that social systems unlike ours may have operated in the past.

This chapter examines the sociology of Grasshopper Pueblo. We can think of sociology as the study of individuals and groups in a community and the ways they interact with each other. Grasshopper society was an aggregate of individuals, each bound by an invisible network of relationships to other individuals and to society as a whole. Human interactions are determined by our various statuses and the roles that accompany them. Status, or social identity, can be thought of as a quality or a condition that may be biologically or culturally defined, such as gender, occupation, political party, marital status, and ethnicity. A role is the behavior associated with a specific status, and it is always defined in reference to interactions. Consider how the same person will behave at a parent-teacher conference, a softball game, and a political party meeting, and you will have grasped these concepts.

This chapter looks at the building blocks of Grasshopper society—individuals and groups—and the glue of interactive relationships that held society together. We begin with the smallest unit, which is the individual. We then move to larger groups, looking at households, the center of domestic life; residence groups, spatial units formed of groups of households within the pueblo; and ethnic groups, broadly defined in terms of cultural affiliation. Along the way we will consider status and role. Our interpretation of Grasshopper sociology is that it was organized on principles of kinship, age, gender, participation in religious life, and ethnic group membership.

Our understanding of Grasshopper Pueblo society comes from analysis of three sets of archaeological information. These are the artifacts and features from room living surfaces, mortuary practices, and human biology. We will turn to these sets of data throughout this chapter.

The Path of Life from Birth to Death

We view the life cycle of the individual as a path leading each person through several different phases of growth and personal change, in which he or she acquired new sets of social identities, roles, and relationships. The most important transitions no doubt were marked by appropriate rites of passage. About most of these we can only make educated guesses, because these important milestones left few traces in the archaeological record.

Birth was the first milestone, marking entry into the sphere of human relationships. We cannot know how birth was celebrated by the people of Grasshopper, although most Pueblo peoples bathe the newborn ritually and, after an appropriate time, give the child a name. We do know, however, that the full nine-month gestation period was recognized, because premature babies were treated differently at death than full-term infants.

We also know that concern, even fear, was joined with joy at the arrival of a baby, for the mortality rate was extremely high for children. More than half the people who were buried at Grasshopper Pueblo had died before reaching their twelfth birthday, and one-fourth were children less than one year of age. When intestinal and respiratory illnesses were coupled with the poor nutrition and food shortages that were endemic, the effects on infants were devastating.

Babies were kept securely and comfortably in cradles until they were toddling about. Differently made and sized cradles were used, depending upon the child's age, if we can generalize from those found at Canyon Creek Pueblo. Haury suggested of the Canyon Creek cradles that they were carried horizontally under the mother's arm, with a carrying strap over the shoulder. Soft shredded fiber or bark served as diapering material, and the baby was wrapped in blankets in colder weather. A bundle of soft grass served as a pillow. Cradles no doubt were carried as the mother traveled to the fields, to gather wild plants, or to fetch water, and they could be placed in sheltered spots out of the weather.

We think that the type of cradle used was culturally determined. Securing the infant inside a cradle created an artificial flattening of the skull from the pressure on the soft, unfused bones. Anasazi and Mogollon people exhibit different types of skull flattening from cradle use. Indeed, this is one way we can differentiate between Mogollon and Anasazi people living at Grasshopper Pueblo. The soft, flexible construction of Mogollon cradles and the way they were carried produced a gentle flattening of the skull in the occipital region. The Anasazi cradles created a more pronounced skull flattening. They must have used a cradle with a more rigid frame or one that was carried in a different fashion. Or they may have used a harder wooden "pillow" to support the child's head. The skulls of Anasazi people are flattened higher on the skull, in the lambdoidal area.

Some time after about age four, the child's world widened as he or she began to play a more active role in domestic group affairs. Children no doubt shared in household responsibilities appropriate to their age, tending younger brothers and sisters, helping with wood collecting, and performing similar chores. This also was a time of better health and less risk of dying for Grasshopper's children, perhaps due to the shift to an adult diet after weaning. A person who survived childhood had a good chance of living another couple of decades.

Between the age of nine and fifteen, the children of Grasshopper Pueblo reached another life-cycle milestone—they achieved adult status. We use a marked change in the burial ritual, from interment beneath a room floor to burial outside of the house, as a measure of this milestone. We think that this shift in mortuary treatment indicates that a young person was considered to be a fully participating adult member of the Grasshopper social and ceremonial community. The circle of relationships widened, extending from the family to include people who were not related by birth. At this time, the young people may have been initiated into some pueblo-wide ceremonial organization, perhaps similar to the Katsina religion among the historically known Hopi people. At this age, children also became eligible to join the smaller, restricted societies that structured ceremonial life.

Marriage must have been another important milestone, marking the transition to adulthood with its resulting family responsibilities. The total dependence of the individual on the household of birth shifted, and still more relationships with people outside of the family were forged. We suspect that people married young at Grasshopper, for most people seldom lived longer than about forty years. Again, we do not know exactly how marriage was celebrated, and we do not know the details of where the newly married couple lived. Among many historically known Puebloan peoples, kinship and material goods alike were inherited through the female line, and newly married couples lived with the wife's mother. It is likely that the family group was extended beyond the married pair; several generations, aunts and uncles, and unmarried adults probably composed the large and busy Grasshopper household.

In adulthood people shared the greatest responsibilities in the economic and social spheres and enjoyed the widest set of social relationships. This was the time of most intensive participation in religious life, village government, and family matters. Men and women played different roles in Grasshopper society, however, which we discuss later.

Although adults did not suffer the life-threatening illnesses that claimed the lives of so many children, life expectancy remained low. Among the adults above the age of fifteen, about one-fourth died in their twenties, another one-fourth in their thirties, and almost 40 percent died when they were forty years of age or older. The remainder were young adults age fifteen to twenty years.

What did the people of Grasshopper Pueblo look like? Let us imagine a typical Grasshopper family. We would see people who resemble modern Native Americans in their physical features, but they are not as tall, and they are less robust. Poor diet and the serious illnesses from which the people suffered ensured that few people would reach more than 5 feet 6 inches in height.

Women's string skirts
from Canyon Creek
Pueblo

The women grinding corn at the mealing bins are around 5 feet in height, and they wear string skirts fashioned from apocynum fiber cordage. Their glossy black hair is short, no doubt because women's hair was cut to make strong, supple cordage. A visiting aunt from Canyon Creek Pueblo wears her short hair bundled up and tied with brown, black, yellow, and white cotton string to keep it out of the way. One can barely see that her skull bears the slight flattening of the occipital bones that marks her as born and raised at Grasshopper Pueblo. When night falls, the women wrap woven cotton or apocynum blankets around their shoulders to ward off the chill air. One of the older women is gorgeously adorned with multiple strings of shell beads around her neck, ankles, and wrists. The afternoon sun highlights the shell and bone rings on her strong fingers as they move the mano hypnotically back and forth across the corn. The toddler giggling as he chases a puppy around the smoldering fire wears nothing except a string of shell and stone beads, turquoise earbobs, and a grin.

The men just arriving from a successful hunt are of average height, about 5 feet 5 inches tall. They wear loincloths, woven cotton shirts, and sandals of yucca fiber. Fastened with yucca or cotton ties that form loops for the second and third toes and heel straps, sandals were secure, even on the most rugged ground. In colder weather the men wear moccasins and leggings. Each man's long, straight hair—not used to make household equipment—is bundled at the back of his head, and one man wears a polished, smooth bone hairpin thrust through the knot. A slim young man is probably of Anasazi origin, to judge by the flattening of his head, and he accentuates the effect with his hair knot. He wears earbobs made of tiny turquoise mosaic pieces and three shell bracelets that came from the faraway sea to the south. He hopes this finery will catch the attention of the pretty young woman who smiles at him shyly from inside her mother's house.

At this time in life, an individual's skills were well developed, and many men and some women apparently had taken on roles as skilled craftspeople, shamans, and warriors. Some men were excellent flintknappers, producing arrowheads and other flaked stone tools with such skill that their products may have been sought by others. Still others appear to have specialized in ritual healing as medicine men. A few men were buried with quivers of tipped arrows, signifying membership in a warrior society, which we discuss more fully in chapter 6.

The penultimate milestone along the life path was when a person reached the status of an elder of the community. Older individuals were accorded great respect, to judge from mortuary treatment and burial accompaniments. When older people died, more effort was expended to bury them, and many more offerings, particularly ceramic vessels, were placed in the grave. Around age forty, men and women alike became revered elders of the community, and the social and economic differences separating men and women became less marked. The most important person we encountered at Grasshopper was a Mogollon man between forty and forty-five years old who died without a tooth in his head. Older individuals no doubt were respected because of their tremendous store of knowledge—practical, religious, medical, mythological, and cultural. In cultures lacking written languages, the only means of transmitting information is through speech. Memory and knowledge become vital instruments of survival.

As it is for all of us, the final milestone was death, where the path of life ended. Death was marked, solemnly and sadly, by mortuary rites. Because of its ritual nature, we discuss the mortuary rite more fully in chapter 6. Unfortunately, death often came early for the people of Grasshopper Pueblo. They were not as healthy as people living in large pueblo communities on the Colorado Plateau, and they suffered from one of the highest levels of dental pathology—caries, abscesses, and tooth loss—recorded in the Southwest. This poor health status is in part balanced by the lack of evidence of violence. The health profile is one of a people with chronic toothaches and assorted pains, subsisting on a diet poor in nutrients punctuated late in the occupation by severe periodic food shortages. The overly romanticized picture of healthy people living happily in harmony with nature is not borne out in the Grasshopper record.

Men and Women at Grasshopper Pueblo

Gender defines much of what we do and who we are, and so it was for the people of Grasshopper Pueblo. Men and women evidently performed different roles in Grasshopper society, and there were varied consequences, ranging from tangible economic benefits to differences in prestige and esteem. Each gender was regarded differently and therefore treated differently at death.

The archaeological record tells us little about the tasks that adult men and women carried out. We can speculate from ethnographic studies of living people that women were primarily responsible for household tasks and caring for the children. They probably did much of the wild plant gathering as well. Men likely did most of the hunting, particularly of large game such as deer. Everyday maintenance tasks were no doubt divided among men and women.

The artifacts placed as mortuary offerings provide a glimpse into gender roles. Because the sex of the deceased is known, there can be no better association between material culture and gender. The artifacts buried with the dead tell us that it was primarily men who were the skilled craftspeople, shamans, and warriors. The average man held more social and ceremonial memberships than a woman, and he commanded a greater variety of esteemed skills. Certain symbolic ornaments, probably worn as part of a ceremonial costume in which deceased males were buried, indicate that men participated much more intensively in the religious life of the pueblo, joining religious societies much more frequently than women. Men alone performed the healing and ceremonial roles of shamans or medicine men. Women, by contrast, tended to have important roles in the domestic arena. Objects indicating skills such as basketry and pottery making are found only in the graves of women. Whereas a boy might expect to mature into the leader of a warrior society or become a respected healer, a woman could anticipate becoming a skilled potter or maker of baskets.

Because of these differing roles, adult men were accorded greater prestige than women, if we may generalize on the basis of mortuary accompaniments. Men have many more mortuary offerings than women, and the funerals of men were probably public events attended by many people.

It was difficult to be a woman at Grasshopper Pueblo. For a variety of reasons that we do not fully understand, more women than men died and were buried at the pueblo—three women for every two men. It is possible that, because their tasks took them away from home on many occasions, some men died from accidents or other incidents and were buried on the trail. It does not seem likely that the lower mortality of men is an artificial product of where archaeologists happened to dig, for the pueblo and its component spaces are well sampled. We think it probable that childbirth was largely responsible for the higher death rate of women because of the greater health risks associated with this process. Women died at greater rates than men throughout their lifetime, but the death rate was particularly high for women in their twenties, when we assume most women were bearing children frequently. Few young women today realize the physiological stress of childbirth under the harsh and unsanitary conditions that prevailed in prehistory.

Poor nutrition was responsible for many health consequences of being female. Bone chemistry analysis by Joseph Ezzo has demonstrated that the diets of adult men and women differed considerably. Women consumed a more varied diet that included a greater proportion of wild plant resources in addition to cultivated food plants. Men, by contrast, apparently enjoyed more meat in their diets. Ezzo relates this to traditional gender roles. Men likely did the bulk of the hunting, whereas women gathered most of the wild plant foods. Certainly women who were consuming an all-vegetable diet, even one enriched by various wild foods, would have been more likely to develop anemia and other deficiency diseases. Through time, however, these differences became less marked, as everyone in the pueblo consumed more corn, fewer wild plant foods, and less game.

The Household, Daily Activities, and Rooms

The household is the basic social group responsible for production, consumption, reproduction, and education. In many non-Western societies, it may include a family surrounded by grandparents, aunts and uncles, and cousins. This type of household is flexible, with the more distant relatives moving in and out of the core group as circumstances change. In other societies, the household may consist of sisters and their husbands and children.

So it was at Grasshopper Pueblo. The basic social group was the household. Households functioned in matters of social control and discipline, as well as in domestic concerns, and were linked through kinship ties and sharing of ritual spaces. There are four activities that every household must perform regularly, in addition to procurement of resources and self-replication. These are (1) habitation activities associated with food preparation and consumption; (2) storage of food, raw materials, and equipment; (3) manufacturing; and (4) ritual activities.

Household activities were carried out in rooms and outdoor areas. Room space was divided vertically; households used room floors—and there may have been more than one if the room was more than one story in height—and also rooftops. Although outdoor spaces and rooftops were used in daily life, it is room floors that provide us with the strongest evidence for identifying domestic activities. In most cases, the artifacts and facilities were best preserved on these surfaces. Although they were work areas equal in importance to ground-level room floors, second-story rooms and rooftops are difficult to identify archaeologically. Roofs typically collapsed when the pueblo was abandoned, mixing artifacts and facilities once intact with things left on the floor, refuse, and construction materials from the collapsing room. Outdoor activity areas are even less readily identified. Few artifacts were left on plaza surfaces, which were less secure than interior spaces, and they were not protected from the elements.

Although every *household* carried out all of their vital support activities, their *houses* used different sets of rooms and activity surfaces within and outside of rooms. We follow Richard Ciolek-Torrello's lead in recognizing recurrent patterns that distinguish how people used rooms.

Types of Rooms

Each room type represents a particular function, or combination of functions, based on the activities that were once carried out there. We recognize these activities primarily from the portable artifacts and nonportable facilities on the floors of rooms, left behind when the people abandoned Grasshopper Pueblo. Sophisticated computerized analysis of artifacts and facilities by Richard Ciolek-Torrello in his dissertation research was used to create the original room types, modified in subsequent studies.

Generalized Habitation Rooms. The best analogy for these large rooms is that of a modern studio apartment. Evidence of all three important domestic activities—food preparation, storage, and manufacturing—is found in these rooms, thus the label generalized habitation room. Cooking hearths, mealing bins, cooking pots, and bowls indicate preparing and serving of meals. Large corrugated jars reflect food storage, and manufacturing tasks are indicated by diverse manufacturing tools and raw materials. Generalized habitation rooms tend to be found in the outliers and were built later than rooms in the main pueblo.

Specialized Habitation Rooms. Food preparation was the major activity carried out in these rooms, which is why they are labeled specialized habitation rooms. Only limited storage and manufacturing took place in them. Slab-lined hearths indicate cooking, and mealing bins with metates and manos in place indicate grinding of corn and other seeds into flour. We imagine that the women spent a great deal of time in these rooms, grinding corn and stewing beans and meat in sooty corrugated pots.

Storage Rooms. These rooms served a very important function. They provided secure storage for foodstuffs and seeds for next summer's crops over

A generalized habitation room at Grasshopper Pueblo

Field school students Robert Fry (left) and Mark Leone excavate a domestic storage room at Grasshopper Pueblo.

the long, cold mountain winters. Without such storage facilities, an agricultural people will fare poorly indeed. Neither light nor heat was necessary in storage rooms and may even have been detrimental; hearths, therefore, are absent. Architecturally, storage rooms resemble other types of rooms, but they are typically smaller than habitation rooms. There are no mealing bins in storage rooms, indicating that grinding of food did not take place, and manufacturing tools are not found in them. Domestic tools such as manos and metates are found in some storage rooms.

In addition to these features, we recognize storage rooms by quantities of corrugated pots, typically large capacity, in which shelled corn, seeds, dried squashes, beans, and other foods and crop seeds were stored. The storage jars were sealed with plugs of clay, or a bit of hide was stretched over them to keep out bugs, dirt, and moisture. We do not know if the perishable granaries like those at Canyon Creek Pueblo, which likely were used to store corn on the cob and other bulky items, were used in storage rooms. We do know that the stone platforms for clay-covered granaries, such as those found in

the Tonto Basin, are absent. We can imagine a Grasshopper housewife surveying her stores of dried corn, beans, squash, cactus fruit, seeds, and nuts
with satisfaction and relief, knowing that her family will be well fed over the
winter and that next spring's seed crop would be safe for planting.

Storage-Manufacturing Rooms. As the name suggests, the two activities that
occurred in these rooms were storage and manufacturing. Like typical storage rooms, they have large numbers of storage vessels, but unlike such
rooms, the storage-manufacturing rooms also contain abundant manufacturing materials and tools, such as pigments, minerals, axes, and grinding
equipment. These rooms are considerably larger than the typical storage
rooms. It is likely that storage-manufacturing rooms may have had some
special function beyond that of a simple domestic room, perhaps serving as a
storage room and work area for a ceremonial or kinship group.

Manufacturing Rooms. These were specialized rooms, characterized by manufacturing tools, raw materials, and debris. Facilities and equipment for food
preparation and storage are not present. Some of the activities that may have
taken place in these rooms include pottery making (pigments, clays, polishing stones, grinding stones), fashioning arrow points and other stone tools
(antler flakers, waste debris, tools), and making ornamental objects such as
turquoise pendants (raw turquoise, abrading tools). Ethnographic information leads us to suspect that the men of the household must have used these
rooms often to fashion the tools and equipment for daily tasks, and the
women may have used the rooms to make and decorate pots.

Limited Activity Rooms. There are two categories within this room class.
These rooms are somewhat different from the other room types, because they
are identified largely on the basis of what objects are *not* found on the floors.
The distribution of limited-activity rooms throughout the pueblo is irregular. Both types of rooms probably represent short-term or temporary reuse of
abandoned rooms as household conditions dictated.

Limited activity/food processing rooms are extremely small rooms used
for grinding and no other purposes. They contain a mealing bin, associated
tools, and little else. Limited activity/manufacturing rooms are abandoned
rooms that were occasionally used for manufacturing, as indicated by a few
tools and small amounts of debris.

Ritual Rooms. There are also two types of rooms that were used for ritual
activities. Ceremonial rooms contain certain features that indicate ritual

activities but lack the formal architectural characteristics that define a kiva. Kivas are highly specialized rooms that were devoted solely to ceremonial activities. Ceremonial rooms and kivas are discussed more fully in the following chapter.

Types of Households

We identify categories of households based on their size. Households are identified by the ways in which domestic activities were carried out in space and by the number of rooms that they occupied. The size differences between households reflect distinctions between larger, older, and, in some cases, more prosperous families and those that were younger, had fewer children, and had accumulated fewer goods.

Large households occupied more than two rooms. This household typically used a specialized habitation room, plus one or two rooms for storage and manufacturing. The largest households occupied three rooms, including a specialized habitation room, a storage room, and a manufacturing room. Large households are found throughout the main pueblo. Medium-sized households occupied two rooms, a specialized habitation room and a storage room, much like the Puebloan pattern widely recognized by other archaeologists.

In contrast to the main pueblo, households living in the outlying room blocks occupied no more than two rooms. These were a specialized habitation room and a manufacturing room. No storage rooms occur in the outliers, which, we suspect, indicates that outlier households were sharing storage facilities with relatives living in the main pueblo.

Small households occupied only one room, requiring that activities be organized much differently than among households using more than one room. Whereas large and medium-sized households used several rooms, each devoted to a special purpose or activity that together provided the complete range of daily activities, small households combined all necessary activities into just one room space. In the main pueblo, small, single-room households consisted of a generalized habitation room and its associated rooftop. In the outliers, these small households occupied only the floor of a generalized habitation room, which combined storage, manufacturing, and food-processing activities. The roofs of outlier rooms were relatively insubstantial structures of pole and brush, like an Apache ramada, or shade, and could not be used safely as an activity surface.

The different households were not distributed evenly throughout the pueblo. In the main pueblo, there were mostly large and medium-sized households. These constitute more than three-fourths of our sample. By contrast, these households form less than 40 percent of the sample in outlying room blocks. This distribution suggests to us a change through time in the organization of households. The larger, better established, and wealthier households continued to occupy the main pueblo, while newer households—smaller and probably less wealthy—occupied the draftier, more cramped quarters in the outliers. The distribution also may reflect seasonal differences in pueblo occupation. Our suspicion that the outliers were only occupied seasonally, a topic we take up in chapter 7, is supported by the fact that small households are more frequent in the outliers and appeared late in the occupation history of the pueblo.

Additional support for the late appearance of the small household comes from our analysis of cooking hearths. The average size of cooking hearths—the rectangular, slab-lined hearths found on habitation room floors—decreased through time. Most of the later hearths were smaller, and in some cases earlier hearths were remodeled by adding additional stone slabs to make them smaller. We interpret this as reflecting a decrease through time in household size. Presumably, as there were fewer household members to consume meals, the women began using smaller cooking pots. Because the pots apparently rested directly on the slab sides of the hearth, smaller pots required a smaller hearth.

Beyond the Family Hearth

We have discussed family, hearth, and household—those intimate family groupings that are fundamental. There were also larger social groups at Grasshopper Pueblo that are reflected in architecture and other material objects. These are residence groups, neighborhoods, and dual divisions.

Residence Groups

Groups of rooms and adjoining outdoor activity areas together formed residence groups. We think that the Grasshopper folk were attuned to the outdoors and comfortable there, taking their lives and activities into the fresh air whenever weather permitted. A complete picture of daily life requires us to consider the activities that took place outside of rooms as well as inside them, although we cannot include them in our reconstruction of households. Outdoor work areas largely complemented the functions of indoor

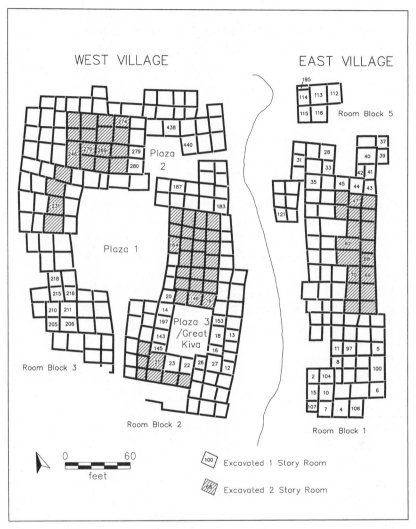

WEST VILLAGE   EAST VILLAGE

Plaza 2

Plaza 1

Plaza 3 /Great Kiva

Room Block 3

Room Block 2

Room Block 5

Room Block 1

0   60
feet

100 Excavated 1 Story Room

68   Excavated 2 Story Room

The main pueblo at Grasshopper

spaces, as different activities took place in each context. There were many advantages to working outdoors, as we shall see. Not all of the activities that took place outdoors left archaeological signatures, however. We suspect that outdoor areas, particularly plazas, were used for socializing and ceremonial activities as well as domestic tasks, but these uses left no traces.

There were two kinds of open-air work areas, distinguished by whether they were bounded by walls or not. These are outdoor activity areas and plazas. Outdoor activity areas were open, unbounded spaces next to rooms. Located on dry, level ground and sheltered from wind and sun by the adjacent rooms, these spaces were ideal for cooking and fashioning tools. Although cooking was common, grinding corn and other foods was not. Mealing bins were never built outdoors. We think that outdoor activity areas were used primarily by household-sized groups and by the women of the pueblo. We can picture them as open-air kitchens, where the women could chat and keep an eye on the toddlers as they watched the stew pot. Activity areas changed constantly over time as new rooms were constructed over them.

Ovens are found only in outdoor activity areas. Ovens were built of masonry, much like a small pueblo room. There are three groups of ovens that we associate with room blocks. One group was found near Salt River Draw in the East Village. A second was located south of Room Block 2, and a third was found beneath rooms in Room Block 3 and obviously had been used long before the rooms above were built. Their capacity and the fact that several ovens are found together indicate that they were probably used by entire residence units. The ovens were filled with rock, so they may have been used much like roasting pits, but there is little evidence to suggest what foods, if any, were prepared in them.

Plazas are distinguished from outdoor work areas because they are bounded spaces, enclosed completely by adjoining rooms, except for an entry. Plazas were the center and the heart of the community. They served a number of mundane functions, but they were much more than this. They were places to socialize, to prepare food for community events, to dance, and to bury the dead. We discuss the ritual functions of plazas in the following chapter.

Domestic tasks that took place include cooking, manufacturing, and refuse disposal. Cooking facilities include roasting pits, firepits, and large slab-lined hearths, some of which were divided into smaller, contiguous hearth spaces. Circular clay-lined firepits may have been used in manufacturing tasks as well as for cooking. There are also large, irregular zones of highly fired clay that may represent places where bonfires were built or pottery was fired. Posthole patterns tell us that cooking and manufacturing facilities were often sheltered by ramadas. We envision women from the neighborhood preparing huge pots of stew to feed people for a feast day, a wedding, or a dance.

Roasting pits were used to steam-bake large quantities of food. A large, deep pit was dug and lined with green grass and branches or any material that would not burn. Fresh corn, cactus fruit, meat, or possibly agave hearts were placed in the pit, which was then filled with rocks. A fire was built inside the pit and allowed to burn to coals, when the pit was covered with earth. The hot rocks and coals baked the food to perfection. We need look only to the size of roasting pits, the quantity of fuel required, and the earth needed to cover them to understand why these facilities are never found in rooms. We also imagine that the succulent pit-baked food accompanied a feast in which a large group participated.

We think that groups larger than single households were the primary users of the plazas, although individual households also used them, and that men and women used them as work areas. The extremely large size of plaza cooking facilities, which have a much greater capacity than those found in outdoor activity areas or inside rooms, signals their communal use.

Like outdoor activity areas, the plazas changed over time in function and intensity of use along with the rooms located near them. Hearths and roasting pits in plazas gradually decreased in size through time or were remodeled into smaller facilities, just like the slab-lined hearths on room floors. Eventually, all of the plazas were converted to ceremonial uses.

Where did the people of Grasshopper dispose of their trash? This is not a trivial question. Specific trash disposal areas helped to keep the pueblo tidy and are important to archaeologists as well, for trash deposits provide us with considerable information about past diet and lifeways. Refuse disposal areas were located outside of the main pueblo and were used only for trash deposition and for burial of the dead. The main midden was located east of the main pueblo; the new channel of Salt River Draw cuts through it today. Other dense trash areas are found south of the pueblo. The plazas and abandoned rooms were also used to dispose of trash. There were no other sanitation facilities at Grasshopper.

Neighborhoods

As we have seen, the Grasshopper community was founded by residents of three separate villages that aggregated to establish Grasshopper Pueblo.

Through time, the three original residence units maintained their individuality, with each room block associated with its own plaza and outdoor activity spaces. Although the residence units cooperated in many activities, they also maintained some social and perhaps ritual independence. Each room block is about the maximum size—between 120 and 140 rooms—of the other large pueblos in the Grasshopper region, each of which also has only one plaza.

The threefold division of the main pueblo into room blocks and plazas continued throughout the Aggregation period and was accompanied by distinctions in architecture, use of fuel wood, diet, and other differences, indicating that the people living in each room block maintained particular ways of doing things that may have been a product of their different origins or affiliations.

The architectural differences among the room blocks are the most obvious. In his dissertation research, Charles Riggs examined the size, orientation, and shape of rooms to discover patterns suggesting that residents of each room block maintained a different building program or style. Room Block 1 has large rooms that tend to be oriented in a north-south direction. Doors are shorter, and little sandstone was used in construction. In addition, double mealing bins are absent, and there are no large storage bins on the room floors. Room Block 2 displays the opposite patterns. The rooms are small, and most of them are oriented east-west. Doorways are large, sandstone was commonly used, large storage bins are present, and double mealing bins are absent. Room Block 3 shares many of the same features with Room Block 2, although rooms tend to vary in size and to be randomly oriented.

Although scant, the evidence points to Room Block 1, which has no formal plaza inside the residence unit, being associated with Plaza 2, Room Block 2 with Plaza 3/Great Kiva, and Room Block 3 with Plaza 1. Each plaza differs in its facilities. Slab-lined hearths like those found on room floors are the most common facility in Plaza 1. Only roasting pits and firepits are found in Plaza 2. This is intriguingly like Grasshopper Spring Pueblo, which also lacks slab-lined hearths, and reinforces the connection with this pueblo to Room Block 1 and Plaza 2. The Anasazi people of Grasshopper Spring Pueblo probably founded Room Block 1 of the East Village. All kinds of facilities were built in Plaza 3, although roasting pits predominate.

We also find interesting differences in the types of wood used to fuel the masonry ovens. Only piñon and juniper—woods that would have been familiar to former residents of the Colorado Plateau—were found in the ovens associated with the East Village. Several types of wood charcoal were found in the ovens associated with the West Village, but oak predominates. These wood species reflect the canyon-woodland zones we suspect were used most heavily by the local Mogollon.

Bone chemistry analysis by Joseph Ezzo reveals that the residents of the three room blocks enjoyed somewhat different diets. Residents of Room Block 3 ate more corn, which might be interpreted as indicating either that they farmed productive agricultural land or that they had a restricted diet that included less meat and wild plant foods.

Dual Divisions

We use information drawn from puebloan ethnography to support an apparent architectural division of the community into two parts—the East Village (Room Block 1) and the West Village (Room Blocks 2 and 3)—which were separated by the old channel of Salt River Draw. Called dual divisions or moieties by ethnographers, the social divisions represented by such architectural separations serve complementary functions in many societies. For example, moieties may divide responsibilities for war from those of peace or allocate community governance into dual organizations, each of which was responsible for tasks according to the season of the year. Often moieties govern ceremonial group membership. Among the Eastern Pueblos, these divisions into Summer and Winter organizations are the workhorses of community life. They organize community religious ceremonies, govern pueblo political life, and direct tasks requiring community labor, such as constructing and maintaining irrigation ditches. The shift from governance by one group to the other is marked by the summer and winter solstices.

It is unclear whether Grasshopper had a moiety organization or what the responsibilities of the divisions would have been, but some intriguing patterns exist in the archaeological record. Among many living pueblo peoples, birds are symbols of clan, moiety, and religious affiliation, as well as central to many ceremonial observances. Charmion McKusick, an expert in the study of bird remains, was the first to observe that birds were not found evenly distributed across the pueblo but occur in spatially distinct clusters. Formal burials of red-tailed hawks, golden eagles, and macaws, remains of blue-feathered birds (jays and bluebirds), and bones of black-feathered birds (ravens and crows) are concentrated in and around the Great Kiva in the West Village. By contrast, formal turkey burials are located in the East Village. Although we consider this inconclusive evidence for the presence of moieties at Grasshopper, the distribution of bird burials does confirm the existence of differences among the room blocks that point to this interpretation.

Ethnic Group Coresidence

Another dimension of group identification was along cultural or ethnic lines. Two, possibly three, different ethnic groups resided at Grasshopper. As we discussed earlier, we identify these groups in the bioarchaeological record by the distinctive types of head deformation produced by different types of infant cradles. The Grasshopper Mogollon exhibit what is labeled vertical-occipital deformation by archaeologists. The Anasazi residing at Grasshopper, like those living on the Colorado Plateau, have the lambdoidal form of deformation. A few individuals without any head deformation may represent a third ethnic group, though they cannot be associated with a particular prehistoric culture. Not unexpectedly, the Mogollon were the majority at Grasshopper Pueblo. The religious leader of the community, the man identified by archaeologists as Burial 140, also was Mogollon.

The Anasazi are represented by a small group of burials, most of whom are women and children. We assume that the women married into the community and that upon their death they were buried there. It is a common practice for women of one community to be given in marriage to men of another community, thereby forging new kinship ties and strengthening social bonds. This time-honored technique was used by commoners and kings alike throughout history to create alliances and extend the network of cooperation beyond blood relatives. It was another means by which the Grasshopper community was able to integrate people with diverse customs and affiliations into a coherent society. The Anasazi mothers, of course, would have used the style of cradle customary in their homeland, creating the signature head deformation among their children.

We think that many of the Anasazi lived in the East Village. Room Block 1 was established by Anasazi people moving from Grasshopper Spring Pueblo. Others may have lived in Room Block 5. This intriguing room block is located immediately north of Room Block 1 and is the only isolated group of full-standing masonry rooms in the main pueblo. T-shaped doorways, which are a common Anasazi architectural trait, and the presence of a particular grave type associated at Grasshopper with Anasazi people are other indications of ethnicity.

The coresidence of Anasazi and Mogollon people in single communities was common throughout the central Arizona mountains. For the most part, these relationships were peaceful and productive. A notable exception is the Anasazi occupation of Point of Pines Pueblo, where, at some point in time, relations between the two groups soured. The Mogollon apparently intentionally set fire to the Anasazi room block, driving the outsiders away permanently. There is no evidence in the archaeological record of Grasshopper to suggest that the Anasazi living there were threatened. Anasazi women evidently married into the community, and Anasazi men joined the same ceremonial societies as Mogollon men, although none were affiliated with the prestigious Arrow Society, the most powerful organization at Grasshopper, which we will discuss in the next chapter.

Household, Kinship, and Grasshopper Society

Although we cannot identify kinship groups at Grasshopper Pueblo, and we do not know the type of kinship system that structured marriage, residence, descent, and other social matters, we are confident that kinship was the foundation of the network of social relations that organized the activities and organization of everyday life. The household was the foundation unit, forming a secure framework for all other social interactions. As it is everywhere in the world, family clearly was vital to survival and happiness among the people of Grasshopper Pueblo.

Yet societies like the one at Grasshopper Pueblo can be threatened to some degree by the same social units that form its core. Factionalism was a typical threat to community cohesiveness among historically recorded peoples in the Southwest. It must have been a particular problem at Grasshopper because so many different groups—kinship, residence, neighborhood, and ethnic—formed a single, diversified community. Ethnography tells us that such societies must develop ways to integrate the different groups to control potential factionalism. The most common method is through marriage. Another is the creation of clubs or societies that draw members from many different households and thus weave a network of relationships that crosscut kinship. The four all-male ceremonial societies that integrated Grasshopper households and kin groups were part of the community religious organization that we discuss in the following chapter. We envision that the entire community, and perhaps even people from other communities, joined together in pueblo-wide ceremonies in the Great Kiva. These activities emphasize the powerful and pervasive role of religion in the everyday life of individuals, households, kin groups, residence groups, and ethnic groups.

Grasshopper Ideology, Religion, and Arts

Religion and ritual pervaded every aspect of life for the people of Grasshopper Pueblo to a degree that modern urban dwellers may find difficult even to imagine. Relying upon anthropology's long history of studying village farmers like those at Grasshopper, we can speculate that the people inhabited a natural world filled with supernatural power and beings, both benevolent and malevolent, that had to be reckoned with in the actions of everyday life. It was not a chaotic world but an ordered one, and to maintain balance with the critical forces of the natural world as well as social harmony it was necessary to follow prescribed rituals.

We think it likely that indeed there was no real, perceived division between the sacred and the everyday worlds and that the Grasshopper landscape embodied and symbolized the sacred. Such a view is maintained still by the Western Apache. Their mountain land is a physical representation of the sacred world. Its places encode many stories and symbols, recording events and people of their mythology, human history, and the interactions of people with the land. As such, the landscape holds the keys to the moral code. To the Western Apache, a particular canyon or mountain is not simply an interesting or colorful bit of scenery but a place where the ancestors acted out a story, and today it retains this historical and spiritual meaning. In this view of the land, plants and animals are not simply objects to be exploited but are related in meaningful ways to history and religion and themselves are spiritual beings. Plants and animals must be used for human purposes with respect and reverence.

For the Western Apache, religion is inextricably intertwined with the ordinary and everyday aspects of life. Ritual binds the two worlds together. So, we think, it must have been at Grasshopper. Archaeologists cannot reconstruct the sacred landscape easily, know the spiritual content of past lives, or re-create the drama of ritual, yet we can convey an appreciation of the central role of religion and the arts in the life of ancient people. We draw our evidence from the sacred spaces where important rituals took place, from the mortuary ritual, and from the well-made, finely decorated pottery that embodied ritual as well as ordinary functions.

Sacred Places

Although we cannot re-create the rich pageantry of the ceremonies that were the cornerstone of community health, well-being, and success, we can identify the areas where they were performed. A multilayered, pervasive religion required both secret and public places for its many rituals and observances.

Why were sacred spaces necessary? We think today of churches, synagogues, and mosques when we imagine sacred spaces, but probably the most important function of religious architecture at Grasshopper was unlike that of modern churches. Secluding most rituals from public view ensured that the sacred remained so. Secrecy is important to much modern Pueblo ideology. When sacred objects and places are profaned by permitting them to be viewed by the noninitiated, their power is lost. Although the need for ritual secrecy probably increased when the Spanish attempted to make the Pueblo people abandon their native religion, we think it existed in prehistoric times as well. We borrow the notion of ritual secrecy and apply it to Grasshopper religious architecture. We suspect that only properly initiated

A ceremonial room at Grasshopper Pueblo

people could participate in and observe the rituals of kivas. It was secrecy that ensured the success of the rites.

In addition, sacred spaces no doubt served a function that was symbolic in embodying particular aspects of the mythology and religion of the Grasshopper people. The architectural features of historically described kivas represent this principle well. They are built underground to remind the people of their place of origin in an underworld, from which they emerged through a hole symbolized by a shallow pit called a *sipapu* in Hopi. Climbing down the ladder into the kiva symbolizes the transition from the mundane world to the sacred one. We cannot know what the architectural features of Grasshopper sacred spaces represented, but we have no doubt that they were physical representations of mythology, cosmology, and legend.

There were five types of sacred spaces: ceremonial rooms, protokivas, kivas, the Great Kiva, and, on certain occasions, plazas. In addition, we suspect that there were shrines and places of power on the landscape that played a critical role in Grasshopper ritual, but we cannot identify them readily.

Ceremonial rooms may be thought of as informal, family-oriented sacred spaces. Although built much like typical habitation rooms, they had special features, including stone-lined ash boxes that may have been used for placing prayer sticks and circular stone hearths. A few storage vessels and manufacturing tools can be found on the floors of ceremonial rooms, suggesting that ordinary activities took place when ritual activities were not being conducted there. There is no evidence for grinding corn or cooking, however, and no indication that people lived in these rooms. Rituals taking place in ceremonial rooms were probably the least formal of Grasshopper's religious activities. We think that three to four households cooperatively used a ceremonial room. No parallel ceremonial structure exists among modern Pueblo peoples.

Protokivas closely resemble similar structures at Chodistaas and Grasshopper Spring Pueblos. They apparently represented an early form of sacred space that was replaced by true, formal kivas. Perhaps the best example of a protokiva is represented by the earliest use of Room 246, one of the first rooms built in Room Block 3. This extremely large room had an earthen platform like the protokivas at earlier sites. It lacked the facilities typically found in habitation rooms, such as cooking hearths, mealing bins, and storage boxes. There is no indication that the room was actually lived in or that food was prepared there. Instead, the room floor was packed with tools and equipment that reflect the fabrication of special objects with ritual significance. Although there also was considerable storage capacity in the form of pots, we think it likely that what was being stored in this room was something other than food and everyday equipment, as in domestic storage rooms.

Describing the floor as it might have looked hints at its special character. One would actually have seen little of the floor, as it was literally covered with objects. The quantity of pots on the floor immediately catches the eye. Although most are corrugated ollas and plates, a few brightly painted black, red, and white pots stand out. Hiding among the larger objects are pinch pots that may have been used to hold prayer-stick offerings. The materials and equipment used to fashion flaked stone tools and prepare arrows, such as shaft straighteners, cores, hammer stones, cobbles, and antler flakers, litter the floor. A closer look would discover finished stone arrow points, scrapers, and knives. Bone ring blanks—deer leg bones from which rings could be cut—indicate that bone ornaments were made there. Polishing stones, manos, metates, and stone slab pot rests attest to other manufacturing activities.

Hinting at curing or other ritual activities are quartz crystals, pieces of gypsum, shell, blue-green malachite and red hematite pigments, and bone whistles, rings, and tubes. There are also everyday tools used in weaving, basketry, and sewing, such as bone awls and antler battens. The observer could not see the several birds that are buried below the floor, including a hawk and two macaws, one of which is covered with limestone slabs.

Perhaps most impressive are seventy-one whole and fragmentary bifaces— large, leaf-shaped stone tools with two flaked sides resembling knives—in various stages of completion. Only a handful of similar items have been found in other rooms. At some of the historic Keresan pueblos of New Mexico, such as Cochiti, Acoma, and Laguna Pueblos, similar flint knives were used in ritual functions, and there was a close association of flint with war.

All of these unusual materials suggest that Room 246 was used to store and manufacture ritual objects. Richard Ciolek-Torrello has suggested that the room may represent the storage and manufacturing area of a clan or moiety. Among historic Pueblo peoples, clans—large groups of people related distantly by kinship—are important units of social organization. Each clan has a large house that serves as its headquarters. The senior woman of the clan resides there, and in it are kept the important ritual objects belonging to the clan. At some pueblos there are also moiety houses, which are used for storing dance paraphernalia, ritual objects, and sacred water. The annual retreats of the leaders and elders of the moiety and the initiations for children are held in the moiety houses. In the Keresan pueblos, the medicine societies have their own houses, which are rectangular structures in the house blocks. Whatever its later function might have been, it seems evident that Room 246, like other such rooms, began its life history as a protokiva with a special ritual character.

Kivas are formal sacred spaces identified by special architectural indicators of religious use. No doubt these features represented symbols in the material world of certain events in mythology and the spiritual world, but we cannot know what these were. A masonry bench across one short wall may have served as a seating area or space for setting up altars and other ritual paraphernalia. A stone ventilator constructed through the bench to open at floor level provided fresh air. These features are absent in all other types of rooms. Other features include a deflector slab placed between the ventilator and hearth to keep drafts away from the flames, a circular stone hearth like those found in ceremonial rooms, and a stone-lined ash box. People did not live in the kivas. No evidence of habitation, storage, or manufacturing activities is found on kiva floors, and there are no mealing bins, cooking hearths, or other features indicating domestic use. Some kivas have holes in the floor that were used to brace the support posts of looms, indicating that weaving was carried out in the kivas at certain times. Formally buried macaws sometimes are found just below the kiva floors, usually behind the bench. Birds, particularly macaws and eagles, play an important role in the ceremonial life of the modern Pueblo people and evidently did so at Grasshopper as well.

A relatively large group of people used the kivas, about twice the size of the small group of households that used a ceremonial room. Each kiva may have been used by one ceremonial society, if we borrow Pueblo analogy. We estimate that six households combined to use each kiva, based on the ratios of habitation rooms to kivas.

Among modern Pueblo peoples, such as the Hopi, the clans own kivas and the rituals performed in them, although membership in the society performing the rituals is open to all, regardless of clan. Kivas serve as crucial sacred spaces for the performance of rituals, and many rituals may be attended only by the initiated members of the society. Kivas are primarily used by men. The kivas are used for weaving when not being used for sacred functions, and men and boys may occasionally sleep in them.

The largest of the roofed sacred spaces was the Great Kiva. It was built when Plaza 3, located in Room Block 2, was fully enclosed by surrounding rooms and roofed. The Great Kiva is particularly interesting, for it reflects a type of group ritual that in earlier times always was more common in the Arizona mountains to the east of Grasshopper. Great kivas were built in places such as the Forestdale Valley, where they may occur in relatively small pueblos, such as the twenty-five-room Tla Kii Pueblo. The construction date of the Grasshopper Great Kiva, around 1330, signals the end of the Aggregation period and the beginning of a period of decreased precipitation, coinciding with population dispersion to satellite communities throughout the Grasshopper Plateau. It is not too far-fetched to believe that the Great Kiva was used as the scene for public appeals to the spirits for rain and abundant crops.

The Great Kiva was, as the name suggests, large in size, about 55 feet long. The roof was supported by massive juniper posts. There was no bench or ventilator. A metate set into the ground was used for grinding white clay, and there was a large firepit near the center. Most striking was a foot drum, a masonry-lined hollow trough into which were set wooden logs or planks. This contraption would create a thundering rumble when struck by the feet of dancers.

No doubt people of the entire pueblo and from neighboring villages as well participated in rituals carried out in the Great Kiva. The Great Kiva brought together in sacred space many people of different kinship, residence, and cultural groups from near and far. Great kivas had long been used by the Mogollon for this purpose and were at one time thought to have been replaced by plazas as public arenas for important ritual functions. At Grasshopper, the three plazas preceded the Great Kiva, and they continued to exist side by side, at least for a time.

Plazas represent the fifth sacred space, one that did not require secrecy or enclosure but was public. Everyone in the pueblo could watch the rituals that took place in the Grasshopper plazas. The cooking and related domestic activities that took place in the plazas were probably associated with the ritual performances. The mountain Mogollon traditionally relied on the plaza as a place to conduct public religious performances. Most Mogollon Pueblo villages of the Arizona mountains are focused on internal plazas, the heart of the village.

Katsina dances at Hopi that we have been privileged to view help us picture the spectacle presented by a ceremonial dance at Grasshopper Pueblo. Imagine the entire village, young and old alike, lining the plaza, sitting on the rooftops, and swinging their legs over the edges as they watched. Masked, costumed dancers, the earthly representations of the spirits, swept through the corridor to appear suddenly in the big plaza, where they danced for rain, health, and harmony. Laughter erupted as clowns made bawdy jokes between dances, and fearsome masked warriors standing at the edges of the crowd kept order and ensured proper respect. The celebration concluded with an exciting free-for-all as the dancers distributed roasted ears of corn, bread, and other favorite foods among the spectators.

The ritual architecture of Grasshopper Pueblo underscores the critical importance of religion in community life, especially under conditions of population aggregation and coresidence of people belonging to different ethnic or cultural groups. An important role of religion was in facilitating decision making by people who did not know one another well during a time of rapid, wrenching change in their way of life.

Ceremonial Societies

Religious personnel were the most important members of the community, for it fell to them to maintain the appropriate rituals for community health and harmony. We think that about half of the adult men of Grasshopper belonged to ceremonial societies that crosscut kinship groups and formed the structural bases of Grasshopper social organization and the foundation of political leadership. We interpret the probable function of these ceremonial societies from living Pueblo peoples, such as the Hopi. Ceremonial societies are devoted to bringing rain and abundant crops, healing the sick, and generally helping the community remain healthy and prosperous. The societies serve to make decisions and resolve disputes, and the leaders of these groups have particularly important roles in pueblo religion and politics.

How do we know these things, when ritual and ceremonialism are so difficult for archaeologists to identify? Our evidence for the presence of ceremonial societies at Grasshopper lies in the artifacts that accompanied the deceased. Some objects occur in graves or were worn by the deceased in highly standardized and patterned ways that would not be likely if these objects were simply ornamental. We think, instead, that these particular objects were worn or carried as part of a ceremonial costume and as such symbolized membership in ceremonial societies.

Ethnography tells us that symbolic representations of identity are common among village farmers, and they are particularly widespread in Puebloan iconography. Animals, colors, and directions symbolize and represent various social groups, including artifact symbols of ceremonial society membership and leadership. For example, the village chief, or *kikmongwi,* at the Hopi town of Oraibi used a wand or stick of authority during important ceremonies. The stick was placed in the grave at death to mark the person as a member of a particular society and a leader in that group. The kikmongwi's face and body were also painted with symbols for important ritual occasions and to prepare his body for burial. Jesse Walter Fewkes, a pioneer archaeologist of the late nineteenth century, states that shell tinklers were considered as socioreligious objects representing Hopi gods.

We have identified four all-male societies at Grasshopper Pueblo on the basis of these symbolic mortuary accompaniments, which are found only with the burials of men. The first society is marked by bone hairpins placed in such a fashion as to suggest that they were thrust through a knot of hair at the top or back of the head. These ornaments are about eight inches long and are highly polished and well worn. A second society is represented by shell pendants made from the bivalve *Glycymeris* shell. These pendants were always found in a position that suggests that the shells were attached to a belt or loincloth.

The third ceremonial society is identified by tinklers made by grinding the tips of univalve *Conus* shells and drilling them for stringing. The bell-shaped tinklers could be strung together in groups, creating a pleasant tinkling

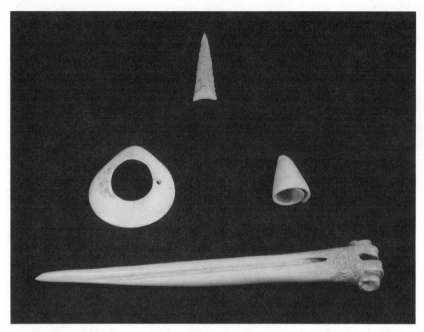

Men's society emblems: an arrowhead (top), a shell pendant (middle left), a shell tinkler (middle right), and a bone hairpin (bottom).

sound when the wearer moved. By their location in burials, tinklers decorated quivers, were sewn to clothing, and, in one case, decorated the tip of a painted wooden staff.

The fourth men's ceremonial society is the Arrow Society, identified by a quiver of arrows placed in the grave. Position and placement indicate the original form, although the perishable quiver and arrow shafts had disintegrated long ago. What remained for archaeologists to find were the stone arrow points, clustered closely together above the left shoulder, with the tips projecting upward. The quiver likely was made from deerskin, cloth, or basketry. We can reconstruct its original size and shape from other objects. For example, a bone rasp in one quiver parallels the original position of the disintegrated arrows, and a circle of shell tinklers on another must originally have been sewn around the opening. Similar quivers of perishable materials, such as leather and cloth, have been found with burials recovered from protected cliff dwellings and rock shelters in the southern Arizona desert and the Verde Valley. Designs on Mimbres Black-on-white vessels depict warriors dressed for battle, protected by a shield, and carrying quivers at the shoulder, with the tips of the points placed upward.

Their limited distribution suggests that the quivers do not simply represent the everyday equipment of hunters. Only seven men at Grasshopper Pueblo were buried with quivers, less than 10 percent of the male burials. We think that most or all men hunted, as indicated by the large quantity of mule deer bones and John Whittaker's study of arrow points and their manufacture. Whittaker concluded that each man made his own arrows and other hunting equipment. Thus, in life the bow and arrow would have been an essential weapon used by all men, yet in death this weapon accompanied only a select few men. The bow and arrow, then, took on a special symbolic meaning in the mortuary ritual.

Support for the interpretation that arrows symbolize ceremonial society membership comes from Hawikuh, the Zuni pueblo encountered by the Coronado expedition in the summer of 1540. In a Hawikuh burial uncovered by the pioneer archaeologist Frederick Webb Hodge, there were three bows and two flutes, and near the left shoulder were seven small arrow points. Also on the left side of the body was a mass of arrow shafts. The quiver was made from a woven material that left an impression on the bows. Watson Smith and his colleagues, who reported these findings, write, "An old Zuni says these are the remains of a Priest of the Bow."

A drawing, from a Mimbres Mogollon bowl, of a warrior with a quiver of arrows that is similar to those used in the mortuary ritual of the Grasshopper Arrow Society.

If our interpretations are correct, there were four men's ceremonial societies at Grasshopper. These were the Arrow, Shell Tinkler, Shell Pendant, and Bone Hairpin Societies. Of course, these are archaeologists' names, taken from the objects that symbolize the society. We have no way of knowing what the Mogollon people called these societies in their own language. Three societies were mutually exclusive in membership, that is, a man might belong to only one. We think this because the shell ornaments and bone hairpins were not worn together. For example, if a man was buried with a bone hairpin, he did not have a shell pendant or tinklers in his grave. This would be an unlikely pattern if the ornaments were just that. The Arrow Society evidently recruited men from all three of the other groups, because men buried with arrow quivers also were wearing tinklers, pendants, and hairpins. Mogollon men belonged to all four societies, but Anasazi men were members only of the Bone Hairpin and Shell Pendant Societies.

Burial 140 at Grasshopper suggests that ceremonial societies were the foundation of political authority there. Widely characterized by archaeologists in earlier years as a high status male, this man does represent the richest burial ever discovered at Grasshopper, but it was wealth of a distinctive and uncommon kind. We think that the abundance and character of the offerings left with Burial 140 reflect his leadership of two Grasshopper ceremonial societies, the Arrow and the Bone Hairpin Societies, and the prestige and authority stemming from this role.

Burial of a Society Leader

Burial 140 was a male aged between forty and forty-five years at the time of his death—given the typical short lifespan at Grasshopper, certainly approaching the status of an elder in years. He was buried in Plaza 3. His grave was covered with a pole roof, built much like the roof of a pueblo room but less substantial. There were two layers of offerings, one placed next to his body and one on the pole roof.

Although the thirty-six ceramic vessels and other objects in this burial are certainly striking, it is the unusual character of the other accompaniments that indicates this man's special position and role. At his head, where no doubt they originally ornamented his hair, were several decorated and carved bone hairpins, including one with a turquoise and shell mosaic handle. Above the head was an elaborately incised and painted wand or bull-roarer made from the femur of a grizzly bear. The decorated hairpins are unique at Grasshopper (no others have been recovered from mortuary or domestic contexts), and few such wands have been recovered anywhere in the Southwest. We think that the striking hairpins, which would have been highly visible when worn, symbolized leadership of the Bone Hairpin Society.

Placed at the man's right shoulder was his personal quiver. Remaining was the cluster of arrow points, oriented with tips pointing upward. The unusual placement at the right shoulder—all other quivers occur at the left shoulder—may perhaps signify that the man was left-handed. A notched bone rasp was carried in the quiver along with the arrows.

Scattered among the two layers of offerings were about 130 arrow points, singly and in clusters. A large cluster of points was placed at the right ankle, and smaller groups of points were placed along the body. In the upper layer were fifty-four arrow points, forty-eight of which were arranged in clusters of two to eight points. Ground specular hematite, looking just like sparkling purple glitter, was sprinkled among the arrow point clusters. Completing his offerings were a stone mortar, whole shell cups, and relatively plain objects, such as undecorated bone awls. The man also wore eight *Glycymeris* shell bracelets around his left upper arm.

The unusual character of the burial accompaniments indicates to us that Burial 140 may have been the leader of the Arrow Society as well as the Bone Hairpin Society. The incised wand and bone rasp probably represent symbols of authority. In all, the rare objects and the emphasis on the symbols of society membership seem to reflect factors other than personal adornment or wealth.

We think that the arrow clusters were contributed by members of the arrow society as offerings. John Whittaker's analysis of these arrow points led to the interpretation that they represent between twenty-five and thirty individual flintknappers. We can picture the funeral of the man we call Burial 140 as a public event, carried out and attended by members of the Arrow Society, each of whom placed a handful of his arrows in the grave as a token of sadness and respect. With great solemnity, with prayers, perhaps with chanting and drumming, the great man was sent on his journey to another world.

Anthropologist Leslie White describes death rites at Zia Pueblo in New Mexico that illuminate the burial of this man. Dr. White writes, "If the deceased was a member of a secret society the head man of the society is notified immediately after death occurs. He notifies all the members of the society, and they gather in the ceremonial house to prepare the costume and paints for the deceased. When they are ready they go to the home of the deceased and prepare him for burial: they put on his ceremonial costume, paint him, and wrap him in a blanket." Four days after death, one of the four societies qualified to perform mortuary ceremonies will conduct a ritual for the deceased. The ritual will be carried out by the deceased's own society if he was a member of one of the qualified societies or by one of the other societies if he was not. The ceremony involves meal paintings, food offerings, and prayersticks and concludes with a meeting in the society house.

Leadership, Authority, and Ritual

The rather clear picture we see of Grasshopper leadership and community decision making is one of male religious leaders assuming authority by virtue of membership in ceremonial societies and probably also kinship. Society leadership may have been bestowed on the individual who had demonstrated the most skill in the performance of ritual, social, and economic activities. It may have been inherited along with clan membership or by virtue of age and kinship position, as in some Puebloan groups. There is no evidence at Grasshopper for any type of true political authority divorced from ritual and kin memberships or for coercion. Except in the midst of hostilities, or when the defense of the community was at stake, decision making was probably based on developing a consensus. Enforcement no doubt relied heavily on religious sanctions and the threat of banishment from the community, a sentence of certain hardship if not death.

If prestige and wealth can be measured by the number of burial accompaniments, then the men belonging to ceremonial societies were accorded great respect and had perhaps accumulated more personal wealth than men who did not belong to such groups. The average number of accompaniments is far greater than among adults as a whole, and the number of ceramic vessels is particularly high. There were evidently some social rewards to accepting the duty of maintaining community harmony and well-being.

The higher social and religious rank of ceremonial society members evidently was not accompanied by real economic benefits, however. Based on strontium, barium, and stable carbon-isotope ratio values, Joseph Ezzo infers that the diets of society members did not differ from those of other adult males. This is another bit of evidence telling us that there was no bona fide social ranking, ascribed status, or stratification at Grasshopper Pueblo.

Ritual, Symbolic, and Artistic Expression

The refined aesthetic sense and the artistic skill of the resident American Indians always impress visitors to the Southwest. Although few have achieved the fame of R. C. Gorman or Allan Houser, many Native Americans, young and old alike, have artistic talent.

The native southwesterners of the past shared the talent we admire today, and the people of Grasshopper possessed artistic skills in abundance. The Mogollon, having settled into a stable village routine, found more time and opportunity to express their artistic sense, and they learned new techniques from the Anasazi.

To understand Mogollon artistic skills, we need to think of art differently from how it is viewed today. In modern times, we conceive of art as creative expression for its own sake. This notion was not common in the past, as far as we can determine. Traditional arts among modern southwestern Indians are time-honored crafts—expertly made, tightly coiled baskets, hand-woven wool blankets that require months of spinning and weaving time, and well-fired, stunningly decorated pottery. The artisans of the past, much like to-day's Navajo, Hopi, and Zuni craftspeople, tended to combine the functional and the decorative. We suspect that the Mogollon expressed their artistic skills largely in fashioning and decorating objects of everyday use. Yet art also had a deeper meaning for the Mogollon that is less readily apparent than the skill with which they made and decorated pots. Much art held symbolic and ritual content and served as a bridge between the mundane and the sacred worlds.

Many of the objects with symbolic significance as well as decorative as-pects, such as cotton textiles, baskets, wooden objects, and other perishable media, have survived only in fragments or in special contexts such as cliff dwellings. Outside of rock art, of which there is little in the Grasshopper region, the most durable remains of their skill are found on ceramics. We use the decoration of Grasshopper pottery as an admittedly incomplete repre-sentation of their art, ritual, and symbolic life.

In discussing this subject, we must be careful to avoid the many interpre-tive traps that await the unwary observer eager to put meaning into a design or to make up a story of the past from a picture on a pot. We cannot presume to know the significance and meaning inherent in ceramics, and we certainly cannot comprehend the ideology and theology on which this meaning was based. Moreover, the specific symbols and message may have been highly personalized. Our approach, therefore, is to reveal some of the finer pieces of this artistic skill and to suggest possible uses and significance when we think the evidence warrants them. We do not interpret the meaning of particular symbols or designs, however, because to do so would be presumptuous. We discuss examples to underscore instead the rich artistic heritage represented

Cibola White Ware pottery from Grasshopper Pueblo

at Grasshopper Pueblo and the strong role art played in ritual contexts—that of objectifying concepts and integrating participants more completely into the values of the community.

Grasshopper had an astonishing array of decorated ceramics. Archaeologists classify ceramics into wares based on how the pots were made and the materials used for the paste, slips, and paints. Each ware has a name that combines a place, often where it was first identified, with a color or other descriptive label. Most of the decorated pottery at Grasshopper can be categorized as Cibola White Ware, White Mountain Red Ware, Roosevelt Red Ware, and Grasshopper Red Ware. Within each of these wares is a series of types that are related through their common technology and colors. These too have a two-part name signifying place and description. Although we stress that these are archaeologists' classifications and labels, it is nonetheless a basic premise of ceramic research that these classifications represented divisions that were meaningful to the potters of the past.

Cibola White Ware represents one kind of the famous black-on-white pottery of the Anasazi. These pots were made from the fine-textured, white-firing clay that is fairly common on the Colorado Plateau but nowhere else in the Southwest. The black paint is made from ground minerals, such as manganese and iron, and the white background is a thin clay slip applied to the surface of the pot. The black-on-white color scheme was retained by firing the pot under conditions where little oxygen was allowed to reach the pot. Black-on-white pots were fired at a fairly high temperature as well. At Grasshopper, almost all of the Cibola White Ware vessels can be classified as Pinedale Black-on-white, and they are decorated in a particular style that was widespread throughout the central Southwest at the time. The Pinedale style consists of geometric shapes, typically interlocking or alternating solid and hatched elements. Sweeping scrolls and keys are common, and the designs almost always have an open center, rather than covering the entire interior of the bowl.

By the time Grasshopper Pueblo reached its peak sometime in the 1320s, Cibola White Ware pottery ceased to be produced in any quantity locally, and none was brought into the pueblo from other regions. This trend was widespread across the Southwest. The black-on-white pots are less common at Grasshopper than other types of pottery. Those we have found are most commonly large storage ollas. We think it likely that these were seldom used for cooking, to judge from the lack of sooting on their exteriors. Small and miniature vessels, most commonly jars and pitchers, also were used as burial offerings.

Most of the decorated pottery at Grasshopper is a red ware, created by slipping the pot with an iron oxide, limonite, or other red-firing slip. To achieve this color, the pots were fired under conditions where oxygen was abundant. There are three major red wares. White Mountain Red Ware is the most spectacular pottery at Grasshopper and occurs in various color combinations and several decorative styles that changed through time. Some pots are painted with black designs on a red slip, whereas others are polychromes that combine black and white paints on a red slip or, in the latest types, black on white and red slips in various combinations. Archaeologists label these types, from earliest to latest, St. Johns, Pinedale, Cedar Creek, and Fourmile, which can be either black on red or polychrome.

These well-made ceramics are similar to Cibola White Ware in technology and materials. Originally yellow in color, the limonite slip changes on firing to deep orange-red. Some unfired pots have been found that bear the original yellow-hued slip. Bowls are the most common vessel form. Few pots have been found on room floors, but many have been recovered in mortuary contexts. We think that the light-paste, well-made White Mountain Red Ware pots were probably not made at Grasshopper Pueblo but somewhere north of Grasshopper on the southern fringes of the Colorado Plateau. Others with

White Mountain Red Ware pottery from Grasshopper Pueblo

identical slips, paints, and decorations have a brown paste that suggests they may have been made locally.

The style of decoration in White Mountain Red Ware is dominated by Pinedale style in the earlier pots and Fourmile style in the later ones. The latter is a flamboyant, asymmetrical style that covers the interior of bowls and combines highly stylized life forms with geometric elements and filler. Although it is certainly subjective, many interpret the designs of Fourmile Polychrome as birds, possibly macaws. We have noted previously the importance of birds, especially macaws, to the Mogollon. Fourmile Polychrome bowls stand out as a particularly fine example of artistic expression and ritual symbolism.

Roosevelt Red Ware, called Salado Polychrome by some archaeologists, is typically associated with the Salado Culture, the late prehistoric pueblo culture of central and southeastern Arizona. It was originally named by archaeologists at Gila Pueblo for Roosevelt Lake near Globe, Arizona. The hallmark of Roosevelt Red Ware is a raspberry-red exterior slip. The black paint is an organic concoction, likely made from a plant such as bee weed or mesquite beans, boiled down to a thick syrup. We do not know the composition of the white slip. The pots were generally fired at a much lower temperature than either Cibola White Ware or White Mountain Red Ware to avoid burning off the organic painted design, and thus they are not as durable as the higher-fired pottery. Most of the pots are made from the coarse, brown-firing clay that is common throughout the Arizona and New Mexico mountains. We think that, like those at Chodistaas Pueblo, many of the Roosevelt Red Ware vessels were made at Grasshopper, but there is sufficient diversity to suggest that others were made elsewhere. Roosevelt Red Ware occurs almost exclusively in mortuary contexts.

Roosevelt Red Ware occurs in several common color combinations. The earliest type is called Pinto Black-on-red, and there is a variant with a pretty salmon-colored slip on the interior. Pinto Polychrome, decorated with black paint on a white interior slip, came soon after. Many, if not most, Pinto Black-on-red and Pinto Polychrome pots were decorated in a style that is virtually identical to that seen in Pinedale Black-on-red and Pinedale Polychrome pots.

Gila and Tonto Polychromes are the latest Roosevelt Red Ware types. Gila Black-on-red, which lacks the white slip, is much more rarely found. Gila Polychrome can also be found with the salmon pink interior slip. Some pots are wildly inventive, using pink, white, and red slips in interesting combinations, but these are rare. There is extraordinary diversity in design in Gila

Roosevelt Red Ware pottery from Grasshopper Pueblo

Grasshopper Red Ware pottery from Grasshopper Pueblo

Polychrome. Some styles resemble other regional decorative traditions, but others appear to be unique. Although a few of the later vessels show stylistic resemblances to Fourmile Polychrome, this style was not wholeheartedly adopted by the makers of Roosevelt Red Ware. Instead, they developed a unique style that has great resemblance to pottery made at Casas Grandes in Chihuahua, Mexico.

The third red ware found at Grasshopper Pueblo is Grasshopper Red Ware. This pottery seems to be unique to Grasshopper. It was made there, and little Grasshopper Red Ware pottery is found at sites elsewhere in Arizona. Grasshopper Red Ware combines the manufacturing technology and materials of Roosevelt Red Ware with the designs of the Pinedale and Fourmile styles. This pottery is generally coarse in texture and was made from a brown-firing clay. Like Roosevelt Red Ware, it was fired at low temperatures. Many pots are thick-walled and heavy. There are black-on-red and several polychrome variants of Grasshopper Red Ware. Less well made and decorated than either Roosevelt or White Mountain Red Ware, the finished product is rather unsophisticated by comparison, although it may have served as a relatively good imitation of Fourmile Polychrome when it was newly made. Of the three red wares, Grasshopper Red Ware is the only one to occur with any frequency on room floors.

This leads us to consider the function of decorated pottery. We think it likely that all of the decorated bowls and perhaps also the small jars were manufactured with the intention of being used in rituals. Why do we think this? As we have seen, most of these vessels were recovered from mortuary contexts, where they may have been placed as offerings or containers for food and water. Many of these mortuary vessels display no wear that would indicate their use as serving dishes or other domestic functions.

The mortuary context of painted pottery is an important signal of its ritual use. There is a domestic set of pottery that occurs on habitation and storage room floors. Predominantly these are undecorated vessels, such as corrugated ware, although there are a few unpainted, red-slipped pots. This inventory of household cooking and storage pots generally does not include White Mountain Red Ware, Cibola White Ware, or Roosevelt Red Ware. Yet this pottery, particularly Fourmile Polychrome, is abundant as potsherds on the surface of the site and in trash contexts. We think that decorated pottery was used in public rituals that took place in the plazas and involved the whole community. The fact that Fourmile pottery is found at small as well as large sites suggests that it was not limited to a particular elite segment of society, as some archaeologists have suggested, but was part of a ceramic inventory available to all. Again, we think that this availability signals its ritual use.

We have long thought that the best single indicator that decorated pottery served a public ritual purpose was development of exterior designs on White Mountain Red Ware bowls. This process paralleled the aggregation of people into pueblo communities throughout east-central Arizona. There is a developmental sequence in exterior decoration through time that signals its increasing importance. Exterior decoration first appeared in the 1100s on a type labeled Wingate Polychrome. The designs are large, bold, solid white decorations, although not all pots had this exterior decoration. Next to appear was the consistent use of broad-line decorations on St. Johns Polychrome, followed by the appearance of an isolated motif or emblem in black, white, or both colors on Pinedale Polychrome. Finally, a continuous band of design in both colors appeared on Cedar Creek and Fourmile Polychromes.

We do not know the message these exterior designs carried. It might have been a traditional sign understood by all who attended the public events at which these pots were used, or it might have been a simple way to signal a household's contribution to a ceremony where food sharing was an integral part of the commitment to cooperation and community harmony. This cooperative effort need not have been any more complicated than a church potluck supper, yet it could have been as rich in ritual symbolism as a sacrament.

Returning us to the concept of secrecy in ritual is perhaps the most comprehensible sign that decorated pots were used in sacred activities—their interior decoration. The symbol-rich designs of decorated pots always occur on the interior of vessels. These designs could not be seen when the pots were filled with cornmeal or pollen. And if the bowls were empty, then only a few people would be privy to the message. It is for this reason that we suspect that the message was limited to a highly personalized exchange between the giver and the recipient, who in many cases was deceased.

Mortuary Ritual

The path of life ended in death, and this solemn event was observed with respectful and formal rites. We suspect that the mortuary ritual was important for a number of reasons. Chief among them, as anthropologists have speculated for many years, rites at death help the living adjust to the absence of their loved ones. The mortuary ritual also was necessary for the deceased, to prepare him or her for the journey to the afterworld and afterlife.

It is important to recognize two points about mortuary ritual at Grasshopper Pueblo. There was, first, a basic ritual, a variation of which was used for everyone, regardless of age or gender. This fundamental ritual can probably be traced to the people's heritage and no doubt reflected their core beliefs about the cosmos, life and death, and the spiritual beings who inhabited the universe. Second, the mortuary ritual was a symbolic and material image of who the living person had been in life. It mirrored the positions and statuses that the deceased person had held—age, gender, family connections, ethnic identity, ceremonial memberships, residence, and special skills. The mortuary ritual also signaled the less tangible factors of prestige.

The fundamental mortuary ritual began with burial of the dead in simple, hand-dug grave pits. This practice was shared by the Anasazi but not the Hohokam of the Arizona desert, who cremated their dead. We interpret the ritual to have been much like the following. Family members, or perhaps members of a man's ceremonial society, dug a simple, rectangular grave pit. This took place indoors or outdoors, depending on the person's age. If inside a room for a child, the grave usually paralleled the room walls and was therefore oriented north-south or east-west. Graves dug outdoors for adults were more varied, although the majority were oriented east-west. The deceased was then dressed in his or her best clothing, which for a man might be the special costume of the ceremonial society to which he belonged. The body may have been washed and painted first, but there is no way to know this. Jewelry was placed on arms, wrists, ankles, and ears. Sometimes the body was also wrapped in blankets or woven reed matting. The deceased was then carefully placed in the grave. Although there is some variation, most often the position was on the back, with legs straight, arms parallel to the body, and head to the east. We think it likely that the orientation of the burial reflected some important event, perhaps the time of day or the position of the sun, or was associated with some affiliation held by the deceased that was symbolized by a direction, but we cannot know.

Then, the deceased's most special belongings were reverently placed in the grave next to the body. Lastly, the people who were closest to the deceased person—family, friends, members of a man's ceremonial societies—placed offerings of beautifully decorated ceramic bowls and tiny jars, which no doubt held food and water, next to the head, feet, or hips. These would sustain the dead person on the journey to the next world. If we can use these ceramic offerings as a measure of anxieties of this world translated to the afterlife, then food and sustenance were central to the passage to a world free from pain and hunger. As a final gesture, powdered pigments might be scattered over the remains and offerings. The grave was then covered, and the ritual was over. No doubt solemn and beautiful words and prayers accompanied these actions, but again we cannot know what these were.

The accompaniments placed with the deceased did not reflect the entire range of objects that were used in everyday life at Grasshopper Pueblo. There were no manos or metates, which the women used daily. There were no cooking or storage pots or the stone tools used constantly for so many tasks. Only ceramic vessels, most of which were decorated bowls, personal ornaments, and a few other special possessions accompanied the dead. We conclude from this pattern that it was the social and ceremonial memberships of the deceased, rather than their daily roles, that were reflected in the mortuary ritual.

This was the standard form of the burial sacrament. Variations in this ritual depended on the social and ceremonial memberships of the deceased, but we look to the path of life to explain much of the variation. How one was treated in death depended largely on whether one was a child or an adult, a man or a woman.

Children in Death

Of all the people living at Grasshopper Pueblo, children held the fewest memberships and performed the most limited roles. Their feet were just setting out on the path of life. Their funerals were therefore family rituals, carried out and attended by their immediate families. Children were buried informally, in less standardized ways than adults, as if each family in this culturally mixed, large community buried their children in the way that was most familiar and customary with their kinship or ethnic group.

Most children were buried within rooms, implying that their funerals were not public events. The youngest infants and stillborn babies were often placed just below the floors of occupied rooms, and the graves were covered with flat stone slabs. The grieving mother may have done this, as did the Hopi, so that the child's spirit would return immediately as another baby. Evidently the people did not fear the spirits of the dead children.

Full-term and preterm infants were treated differently. Most of the burials found in trash areas without a formal grave pit are fetal burials. Ceramic offerings are seldom found, and there is no decorated pottery with these burials.

Graves of children, particularly those under four years of age, were often covered with stone slabs, or the entire pit was lined with stone to form a cist. Babies at Canyon Creek Pueblo were buried in their cradles, and we suspect this was also true at Grasshopper, but the perishable cradles did not survive over time.

Although children were placed with care in the grave, their bodies were positioned in many different ways, occasionally with the legs bent rather than extended and often with the head placed in a direction other than the east. Again, this suggests that children were buried by members of their immediate families, and we think that this variation also indicates that the youngest children may not yet have been initiated into pueblo-wide ceremonial groups.

In contrast to adults, there is little variability in the artifacts buried with children. Our interpretation is that children held fewer social memberships and possessed fewer skills than did adults. Children did not belong to the ritual societies of their elders, and they had not yet had the chance to mature and gain acceptance as parents, leaders, and artisans. Children were dressed in personal ornaments, often strings of stone and shell beads, and occasionally pottery vessels were placed in the grave, but there was little else. The ornaments that we think signify membership in ceremonial societies and the utilitarian and ritual tool kits that accompany adults are not found with the youngest children. Moreover, the offering vessels were less frequently decorated than those placed with adults, and many are miniatures.

We can picture the bereaved family, saddened by the loss of yet another child, tearfully dressing the baby in strings of colorful beads, placing the child in the cradle, and leaving in the grave a beloved tiny pot. It is in the variable treatment of children that we gain a sense of the importance of family and of the sadness and the inevitability of death in a community where more than half its members were destined to an early death.

Adults in Death

If children were the future of the community, adults were its present, and they maintained life in the pueblo. Fully in the middle of life's path, they were parents, society members, skilled craftspeople, and leaders. Their funerals reflected their busy lives and their many roles, and the artifacts that symbolized their memberships in the community were buried with them at death. Their burial outdoors and in highly standardized ways signifies that their funerals were public affairs, carried out by people who were not necessarily closely related to the deceased and attended by mourners beyond the immediate family. The mortuary ritual for adults was formal and almost invariable.

Adults were most often buried outdoors, particularly in plazas. This ensured that the funeral could be attended by as many people who wished. Abandoned rooms were used occasionally for adult burials, but adults were never placed in occupied rooms, as far as we can determine. Physical anthropologist Walter Birkby has suggested that rooms were only used as burial sites in winter, when the ground outdoors was frozen and covered with snow.

Unlike children, considerable energy was spent making the graves of adults comfortable, even elaborate. Some were covered with a wooden roof, like that described for Burial 140. Others, primarily for women, had stone slabs or cists, and still others had additional chambers where the burial offerings could be placed. This can be seen as building a house for the deceased. These elaborations are seen most often with the oldest adults, signifying their individuality as revered elders of the community. Woven reed matting may have been used to line the grave.

Dressed in his or her clothing or ceremonial costume and personal ornaments, the deceased was often wrapped in a blanket or matting and laid to rest. Few adults in the midlife years were buried in the semiflexed and flexed body positions seen among children. This lack of variation and its contrast to the burials of children may be further indications that a group other than the immediate family was involved in the burial rite. Among the oldest adults, there was a return to greater variation in body positions, which may signify their retirement from active participation in ceremonial societies and their burial by the immediate family.

Adults in their prime had developed a repertoire of various skills, and many had achieved positions of importance based on their talents. They were buried with their tool kits. A man buried in Plaza 1 must have been a skilled flintknapper. His tool kit for making arrow points and other tools included an anvil that supported the stone while it was being flaked, several antler-flaking tools, cores of high-quality raw material, the debris resulting from flaking tools, and a few finished tools. We think that another man, buried in Plaza 2, must have been a medicine man or shaman. His collection of ritual objects, which may have been used in curing ceremonies or as symbols of personal power, was found in a tight cluster at his hip, as if the objects had originally been contained in a perishable pouch or bag. In another burial we found clear evidence for such a medicine bag. The pelt of a skunk, with the head and feet still attached, was used to fashion the bag. Archaeologists recovered, of course, only the small foot and skull bones and the objects that were inside the bag. Among the objects found in such medicine kits are quartz crystals, unusually shaped flaked stone tools, marine shells, worked and unworked pigments, animal effigies, curious natural objects such as concretions and fossils, and beautifully fashioned objects with no obvious function, such as polished agate cylinders.

The high regard most adults commanded in the community and their many social memberships were evident at death. Ceramic offerings, particularly decorated pottery, invariably accompanied adults, and certain individuals had numerous vessels. We imagine the friends, family, and ceremonial brothers of the deceased each stepping forward to place a bowl filled with cornmeal, squash seeds, or some other favorite food to nourish the spirit. The number of offerings seems to indicate a large group attending the mortuary rite.

Yet not all adults were alike, and their chief difference was gender. Men and women were treated differently in death.

Men versus Women in Death

The path of life for men and women did not lead to the same place. Each gender performed a different role in Grasshopper society, and each held a different set of group memberships as a consequence. Women's roles centered about the hearth, home, and children, whereas men participated in the wider arena of public and religious life. In death there are quantitative and qualitative differences that reflect these divisions. Adult women were buried in a manner that is somewhere between the high-energy formal ritual for adult men and the low-energy informal burials of children.

For the most part, burial location did not differ between men and women. Almost all adults were buried outdoors, regardless of sex. The standardization in grave type and body position that occurs with men has no parallel in the burials of women, however. The variations in grave type and body placement that occur among women are the same ones seen with the burials of children. These include stone slab covers and stone cists and burial in a flexed or semiflexed position. The parallels between children and adult women imply that, because of their more limited role in Grasshopper society, particularly in ceremonial life, they may have been buried in a less public manner and by their immediate families. Few women were buried in a grave lined with matting or wrapped in some type of body covering.

It is in the number and types of burial accompaniments that the differences between the sexes are most apparent. The average man was buried with about twice the number of artifacts as the average woman, and these objects are also different in kind. Much finely decorated pottery accompanied deceased men—the White Mountain Red Ware and Roosevelt Red Ware we discussed previously and Cibicue Painted Corrugated and Polychrome pottery. The latter pottery, which is decorated with an unusual purple paint, may have been made specifically for use as burial offerings. Women were accompanied by white ware and the less well made Grasshopper Red Ware. The tool kits of skilled craftspeople are accompaniments of men, not women. Only in their personal ornaments are men and women similar, and even these are of different types. Only men wore the ornaments we think suggest society affiliation, such as bone hairpins and shell pendants. Women alone wore shell and bone rings. Rather than suggesting that men were wealthier than women, we think that these differences reflect the more public lives of men and their more formal burial by a larger group, probably the members of the ceremonial society to which a man belonged, as we saw with Burial 140.

No women were buried with medicine bags, flintknapper's kits, or quivers of arrows. Instead, we find polishing, pecking, and rubbing stones and utilitarian bone awls that were not worn as hairpins but placed near the hands, as if ready to weave a basket. This may suggest that a woman's special talents were in pottery making and basketry. If these patterns are representative,

Cibicue Painted Corrugated and Polychrome pottery from Grasshopper Pueblo.

there was a sharp division of labor in the Grasshopper community, and men alone were shamans, flintknappers, and hunters or warriors.

All of this indicates to us that the participation of women in religious life was rather restricted and that the fewer social and ceremonial memberships of women are reflected by a less public mortuary ritual and fewer offerings. This does not necessarily mean that women's contributions were not important or that they were regarded with less respect than men, simply that men's and women's roles were different, and the mortuary rite mirrors this distinction.

Anthropologist Mischa Titiev, in a classic treatise on the Hopi of Oraibi Pueblo, summarizes the basic principles of their religious life in a way that sheds light on how ceremonialism, ideology, and mortuary practices may have been intertwined at Grasshopper Pueblo. He writes that the fundamental concept of Hopi religion is a belief in the continuity of life after death. Significantly, the distinctions between the living and the dead are minimized. The afterworld is a replica of life on earth, except that the dead do not consume real food as do living people. The dead are transformed into clouds, and in these spirit bodies they may revisit the pueblos, where they are represented by Katsinas. The people who prepare the body for burial place a mask of cotton on the face of the deceased to represent the clouds and make him or her light as air. The Hopi say, "You are no longer a Hopi, you are changed. You are grown into a katsina, you are a Cloud." The dead return to the underworld, from where people first climbed up into the living world, through the same sipapu. When they revisit their former homes as clouds or Katsinas, they bring rain, health, good crops, and all manner of benefits to the Hopi. So may it have been at Grasshopper, long ago.

Dispersion and Abandonment Periods

Again it was a time of little rain, dust, and forests burning, but not as bad as before. The snows were not so much and the summer rains fell in different places on the land. Some fields got water and other fields turned to dust, and the deer had gone from Grasshopper. The children cried. There was not much food at Grasshopper, so many people had to move. And the time came when all the people moved away.

In these words the grandmothers of Grasshopper might have remembered the final years at Grasshopper Pueblo—a time of leaving but also one of beginning again. The years at Grasshopper Pueblo had been good, rich years of rain, fat deer, and piñon trees heavy with nut-filled cones. But there came a time, in the middle years of the 1330s, when snow and rainfall once again were scant and what fell was variable across the land, soaking some places and leaving others dry. There followed a prolonged drought lasting until 1355. This was a critical period in the lives of the people. Unlike the earlier Great Drought, when the region was sparsely populated, it was a time of maximum population on the Grasshopper Plateau, and there were immense demands on food resources. The farmland was becoming depleted and the wild plants and animals were no longer as abundant, all because so many people were trying to make a living from the land.

Combined with the poor climate, these factors had disastrous consequences. There were food shortages and nutritional deficiencies as the people increasingly consumed less of the scarce wild foodstuffs and relied even more on corn. Increased physiological stress among children, seen in bone growth abnormalities and anemia, attests to the recurrent food shortages caused by crop failures and the poor nutrition of a corn-dependent diet. The response to these increasingly severe problems was a time-honored Mogollon strategy. They simply moved away. Dispersion—movement away from the central core of the pueblo—began around 1330, and the processes that transformed dispersion into abandonment of the region were complete by 1400.

Two processes are evident during the Dispersion period. Some households returned to a settlement system marked by residential mobility, and numerous satellite communities were established and grew. There is no archaeological evidence to indicate that the Mogollon responded to their agricultural shortfalls by introducing technological improvements such as irrigation to increase productivity—an improvement that would be used hundreds of years later by the Cibecue Apache—or by trading for food beyond the local region. We also look to the building of cliff dwellings, such as Canyon Creek Pueblo, to help us understand the dispersion process more completely. Last, the Great Kiva at Grasshopper Pueblo is mute testimony to the stresses and strains of this time and to the success the people achieved in coping with these difficulties.

Return to Household Mobility

The Dispersion period was marked by a return to the traditional Mogollon settlement pattern characterized by frequent residential moves and seasonal occupation, a pattern that had been interrupted and altered during the Aggregation period. We see this on a large scale in settlements that were established across the Grasshopper Plateau and at Grasshopper Pueblo at a smaller, more detailed scale in changing patterns of room function and occupation.

At Grasshopper Pueblo there was a great contrast between the outliers and the main pueblo during the Dispersion period. The outlying room blocks on the low hills overlooking the main pueblo were largely made up of generalized habitation rooms, where food processing, storage, and manufacturing activities took place. The compression of all daily domestic activities into one room, along with the small cooking hearth, indicates that these rooms were inhabited by younger, smaller, more mobile households, such as young families with few children. Because most of these rooms were built with low walls, having only a foundation of stone and a roof of pole and brush, it is likely that they were used seasonally during the warm months of late spring to early fall. People who wintered over at Grasshopper Pueblo needed the protection of rooms in the main pueblo built entirely of masonry, with their high walls and large hearths, to withstand the cold and snow. Such rooms belonged to the older and larger households, who remained all year at the main pueblo. The storerooms of these households were used by the seasonal occupants of the outliers whenever more substantial facilities were required.

We also see a return to household mobility in the many small masonry pueblos throughout the Grasshopper Plateau that are situated on high landforms and in cliffs. Such pueblos were used initially for part-time habitation and hidden storage. They offered an option intermediate between living full-time in an aggregated village and moving off the Grasshopper Plateau altogether.

Some of these changes reflect simply the normal, natural progression of household development. In its later stages, the older families remained in the main pueblo all year, while the younger families moved seasonally between Grasshopper and one of the small butte-top pueblos or a satellite community such as Canyon Creek Pueblo or Red Rock House. The fact that so many of the generalized habitation rooms in the outliers have a complete inventory of nonperishable artifacts on the floor suggests that the occupants anticipated they would return, but for some reason this did not happen.

Satellite Communities

The second process that took place during the Dispersion period was the establishment and growth of satellite communities in the Grasshopper region. The Mogollon had traditionally adjusted to food shortages by expanding the land under cultivation. This often necessitated some households moving away to establish new villages, a common practice among the historical period Hopi. As households dispersed from Grasshopper Pueblo into smaller patches of more marginal agricultural lands, new settlements arose throughout the Grasshopper Plateau. The siting of some small pueblos on easily defended, butte-top locations, use of secret caves in the security of cliffs to cache and hide food, and three cases of scalping among the burials at Grasshopper Pueblo all suggest that these households, widely scattered across the land, operated in an environment of social and economic uncertainty.

There are ten pueblos on the Grasshopper Plateau of more than thirty-five rooms that were occupied during the 1300s. Together, these pueblos represent the bulk of all the rooms we estimate were occupied at this time and obviously hosted the majority of the population. The pueblos were located near agricultural land and were also defensively positioned along the plateau perimeter. These locational variables support our interpretation that settlements dispersed in order to expand the area for food collecting and to bring new farmland under cultivation. All but one of the largest pueblos, other than cliff dwellings, are either within or overlooking a patch of good farmland, and Grasshopper, the largest of these pueblos, is in the most extensive expanse of these agricultural soils.

These pueblos seem to have been established at different times, implying that the establishment of satellite communities was a gradual process and that each satellite also underwent its own history of growth and development. One line of evidence in support of this interpretation is the developmental sequence in village layout, where rooms are built around plazas. David Tuggle reasoned that Grasshopper Pueblo, as the largest and oldest pueblo, represents the end stage of development, and it has fully enclosed plazas. The other pueblos, therefore, could be arranged according to the degree to which the plaza is enclosed. The order of this architectural sequence is the same as the order of pueblos by size, suggesting that size differences are a function of time of establishment and occupation span or simply age at the time of abandonment.

Moreover, when the density of rooms per square mile of agricultural soil is calculated, the ordering based on density closely parallels the order based on size. This pattern, where smaller pueblos have a shorter occupation span and fewer rooms per unit of agricultural soil, indicates to us that pueblo size is a function of differential establishment and growth through time. These lines of evidence strongly support the interpretation that the largest pueblos on the Grasshopper Plateau were new communities established at different times to expand the agricultural land under cultivation.

Canyon Creek Pueblo, a cliff dwelling on the western edge of the Grasshopper Plateau.

Canyon Creek Pueblo

One Saturday in the summer of 1970, Emil Haury led the field school staff and students on an all-day hike to Canyon Creek Pueblo, a cliff dwelling he had not seen since he spent six weeks excavating there in the summer of 1932. At that time, Haury approached the ruin from the west, riding in with those contrary pack mules described so colorfully by Slim Ellison. And here is what Haury saw, in his own words:

> The site occupies a shallow recess in a sandstone cliff near the head of a short unnamed canyon which enters Canyon Creek about one mile below the mouth of Oak Creek. . . . The floor of the lateral canyon rises gradually for the first mile of its ascent, then rapidly over a series of low cliffs which brings it to the level of the ruin, and, finally, it continues upward in less accentuated form to drain the upland. The cliff which provides the shelter for the ruin . . . is of sandstone, changing in color from red to buff. Its height is about one hundred and seventy-five feet, and its elevation above sea level is approximately six thousand feet. From its foot, a talus slope breaks away one hundred yards to drop over a second and, a little lower still, a third cliff. The ruin is situated about a thousand feet above the floor of Canyon Creek. . . .
>
> The flora is chiefly that of the Upper Sonoran zone; the large trees are pinyon and juniper, pine being somewhat higher up. Sycamores grow along the water courses, and oak and walnut trees occur along the base of the cliff and in sheltered spots. Catclaw is everywhere in abundance, as well as several varieties of cactus and yucca. These, together with beargrass and other grasses, provided the occupants of the village with the needed materials for textiles, sandals, and basketry.
>
> On the talus slope a few yards below the eastern-most end of the large house there was evidence of a seep which may, at one time, have been developed into a spring, but the main source of water in the canyon was a large spring at the base of the sandstone cliff about three hundred yards southeast of the ruin. This spring, prior to the beginning of the rainy season, flowed from fifteen to twenty gallons of clear cold water per minute. It must have been a valuable asset to the community.
>
> Arable land was at a premium. In every direction for several miles the land is so rocky and the country so rugged that agriculture could only have been carried on with difficulty. The bed of Canyon Creek provides relatively few benches and terraces of tillable land; nevertheless, the remains of agricultural products were found in abundance.
>
> About one hundred and twenty-five rooms can be traced in the canyon. . . . Fifty-eight of these are concentrated in a single two-storey structure, the remaining number being scattered in smaller groups along the bases of the upper and lower of the three cliffs. All work was confined to the major unit. . . .

This group has a frontage of about two hundred and fifty feet on an east-west axis. As the recess was forty feet from front to back, it allowed space for the construction of three rooms on a north-south axis. . . . The outermost rooms, due to greater exposure to the elements, have been largely demolished; but those nearer the cliff are still in a very good state of preservation. . . . While a number of rooms have been destroyed by fire, seven roofs still remain intact and five others are partly preserved. In two instances, the roofs and floors of two-storey rooms are in perfect condition. Although the highest standing wall at the present time rises twenty-three feet, there is no evidence that any part of the village ever had more than two storeys.

In 1970 the pack mules were long gone. We parked our four-wheel-drive trucks on Whitetail Rim, the western edge of the Grasshopper Plateau, and scrambled through dense catclaw and mountain mahogany to reach the creek that opened into Ghost House Canyon and the cliffs where the ruins are perched. The enchantment, solitude, and sweeping view of the distant landscape compelled us to return year after year, sometimes simply to treat field school students to this remarkable place, other times to continue the work that Haury had begun so many years before. The founding of Canyon Creek Pueblo illustrates many of the processes we have discussed concerning the relationship of Grasshopper to smaller communities, satellite village formation, and agricultural management during times of drought.

As the overworked land close to Grasshopper Pueblo that so many people depended upon lost its fertility and productivity, it became apparent that people would have to move. They must have anticipated that someday they would move to that sheltered alcove overlooking Canyon Creek, where in the canyon bottom or on the rim above they would find new land to cultivate. Toward that day, they began cutting trees and stockpiling them where their new home would be built. Michael Graves discovered this in an analysis of the tree-ring evidence from Canyon Creek Pueblo, which indicated that many of the roof beams were cut as much as a decade before they were actually used in room construction. We can imagine that some of the newly committed Mogollon farmers of Grasshopper, with memories of the Great Drought still fresh in their minds, were little fooled by the above-normal snow and rainfall that accompanied aggregation at Grasshopper Pueblo and sought to buffer an anticipated crash by preparing for the founding of satellite communities. It seems no coincidence that initial construction at Canyon Creek, which took place in the late 1320s, coincided with peak population at Grasshopper Pueblo and preceded by only a few years the dry spell of the mid-1330s.

Construction at Canyon Creek Pueblo continued at a rapid pace until almost 1350, but the village probably continued to be occupied for many years thereafter. At its peak there were around 120 rooms scattered along the cliff face, with most of them concentrated in the major room block of around 58 rooms.

Everyday life at Canyon Creek was little different from life at the Grass-hopper community the people had left behind and to which they still returned regularly for important social and ceremonial occasions. The food remains that Haury found there, however, indicate the beginning of changes to the diet that would become more pronounced as time went on. Haury found evidence for reliance on farm produce but few wild plant and animal foods. There were abundant corn cobs, red and white beans, and two varieties of squash. Wild plants included only acorns, black walnuts, and yucca—plant foods available in the nearby canyonlands. Hunting seems to have been not as dependable as it had once been. Mule deer, wild turkey, domestic dog, jackrabbit, and two foxes were the only animal bones recovered—a great contrast with the variety and abundance of animal bones at Grasshopper Pueblo. Haury thought that because most of the animal bones recovered were mule deer and wild turkey, this indicated their high food value contrasted with smaller game.

There are no true kivas at Canyon Creek Pueblo, and Haury noted that only Room 22-B, a second-story room, offered any suggestion of ritual use. Haury observed the following features in the room:

> A shallow pit in the south center of the floor marked the fireplace, while in the south wall, two feet above the floor, there occurred the twelve by seventeen inch ventilator already described as having been made by partially filling in a doorway. . . . Directly in line with this wall opening and the firepit was a vertical slab imbedded in the floor. Its length was about twenty inches, its height above the floor eight inches. In the twenty-inch space between the deflector and the wall, there rested a flat stone loosely supported a few inches above the floor by small rocks. This seems to have been used as an altar, for on it were found the following articles: a small unfired animal effigy, . . . a cane arrow with stone point, . . . a bit of textile in which was tied a small quantity of salt, a broken shell pendant, fragments of a black-on-yellow bowl, and two clay legs of other effigies. Elsewhere in the shallow fill of the room, there were found the antler arrow wrenches, . . . parts of a textile bag with design worked out in the process of weaving, . . . a broken jar with a yucca fiber handle, many yucca quids, and quantities of acorn and walnut hulls.

In addition to these artifacts, the walls were decorated in a terrace design in red above a three-foot-wide band of yellow. Terraces are widely recognized as a cloud symbol in the designs of modern southwestern Indians.

This ritual function of Room 22-B resulted from modification of a room that was previously used for domestic activities, as indicated by field school student Toby Volkman's 1972 project. She argues that the room was modified sometime after 1342. We agree with her interpretation that the creation of the ritual room signals a shift from seasonal to year-round habitation late in the pueblo's construction sequence and perhaps also a reorganization of ceremonial life and a return to local control of ritual life, following a time in which the people may have been dependent on Grasshopper Pueblo for their important ritual activities.

The Great Kiva at Grasshopper Pueblo

As we saw in chapter 6, Plaza 3 in the West Village was converted into the Great Kiva sometime around 1330. We do not know when the Great Kiva was abandoned, but we have no reason to suspect that it occurred long before the abandonment of Grasshopper Pueblo. A small number of burials placed into the fill of the Great Kiva indicates that time elapsed between its disuse and pueblo abandonment.

Although it has long been thought that great kivas served to integrate a population, it has been difficult to determine the ecological and social circumstances under which they were constructed and the role they played in the evolution of pueblo religious life. The Great Kiva at Grasshopper gives us insights into these processes. That the Great Kiva was constructed at the beginning of the Dispersion period strongly suggests that the structure was designed to serve as a focal point of ritual activity for those households that were moving back and forth between Grasshopper and satellite communities such as Canyon Creek Pueblo. Because the Grasshopper structure is the only great kiva identified to date on the Grasshopper Plateau, we assume that it served the entire regional population.

The integrative function we think that the Great Kiva performed—one which goes back centuries to the Bluff and Bear Villages of Forestdale Valley—was to gather together in one large structure people of different ethnic backgrounds. This would have been especially important during times of environmental stress, when it would have been crucial to exchange information on rainfall, game availability, or crop yields throughout the region, as well as to coordinate the ceremonial activity necessary for rainfall, fertility, and social harmony.

Abandonment of the Grasshopper Plateau cannot be taken to indicate the failure of the Great Kiva. If one important function of the Great Kiva was to meld different ethnic groups into a coherent society, then the blending of the once-distinct Grasshopper Mogollon culture into a broader cultural pattern essentially indistinguishable from that of the Anasazi is clear evidence of its success.

Abandonment

Dispersion of settlements throughout the Grasshopper Plateau was the first step taken by the Grasshopper Mogollon and those who had joined them during the Great Drought to adjust their population to changing environmental conditions. As we have seen, the initial occupation of Canyon Creek Pueblo was probably seasonal. That these alert farmers clearly anticipated the need to move there suggests that it did not take long to respond to agricultural shortfalls and changing weather conditions. The people were able to quickly mobilize households, taking whatever steps they saw necessary to bring new farmland under cultivation and feed their hungry families. But it was probably inevitable that what began as seasonal moves over short distances extended to more and more time spent away from Grasshopper Pueblo and eventually led to the abandonment of the region.

Options other than moving to new land certainly were available to the people of Grasshopper Pueblo, at least potentially, and could have operated effectively for a short while. The people could have spent more effort on farming their established fields, for example, or trading with folks living elsewhere for food or valued commodities that could be exchanged for food. But we have no evidence that they considered such options. The Canyon Creek case points to the traditional strategy. Farmers sharply aware of changing trends in precipitation knew it was necessary to make adjustments and could translate this rather quickly into short-distance moves. This strategy was well used by the historically known Hopi people. When population and the productivity of their farmland fell out of balance, the Hopi typically responded by moving, first to fields located ever farther from home and eventually to new homes closer to better farmland.

Although they succeeded in managing agriculture during this period of reduced precipitation, the people of Grasshopper were less successful in regulating hunting. John Olsen found that the Dispersion and Abandonment periods were marked by increased harvesting of immature deer compared to the Aggregation period, and deer bones were thoroughly reduced to yield as much food value as possible. When once it might have been possible for relatively small populations in the mountains to defend against crop short-falls by hunting more deer, this strategy did not work under the conditions that prevailed at Grasshopper Pueblo. This practice would actually have reduced the deer population at a time when decreased precipitation was already adversely affecting local herds. In other words, the people hunted themselves out of game.

These were bad times, indeed. Agricultural shortfalls coincided with game management ineffectiveness under conditions of population aggregation during a time when rainfall was low and erratic. The combined effect of these factors was initially to force the people to accept a subsistence strategy totally dependent upon agriculture, as John Welch's research concludes, sometime in the mid-1300s. The Anasazi immigrants who moved into the mountains during the Great Drought introduced more efficient dry-farming techniques as well as ways of adapting to life in large pueblos and probably also a number of religious practices. If our interpretation is correct, then, in the early 1300s the local Mogollon underwent a radical alteration in life-style that brought them closer to living like the Anasazi in subsistence, social organization, and religion. Dry-farming technology, which provides lower yields than irrigation farming, could not sustain the population, however, with the result that the inhabitants responded as they had so often done before. They packed up their belongings and moved to farmland with a more predictable water supply.

By 1400, when the last mountain pueblo was abandoned, the Grass-hopper Mogollon had swapped their traditional emphasis on mobile hunt-ing, gathering, and gardening for the life of the pueblo village farmer. At this point in prehistory, archaeologists lose track of the Mogollon because they became indistinguishable from the Anasazi in the archaeological record. The Grasshopper Mogollon adjusted, changed, and eventually disappeared from the archaeological record of the Arizona mountains.

Where Did the Mogollon of Grasshopper Go?

The Hopi are often amused when a *baha'ana* (Euroamerican) asks about the disappearance of the Anasazi from the Four Corners at the end of the Great Drought. They point out that there *was* no disappearance. The Hopi descen-dants of the Anasazi still populate the Colorado Plateau. They did not disap-pear; they simply moved away. That is what happened to the Mogollon. They moved, but in their case we do not know to where.

There is no evidence for any catastrophic natural occurrence having suddenly destroyed villages. There was no cataclysmic fire, earthquake, or flood. Social unrest and economic uncertainty did not give way to warfare, and chronic food shortages did not lead to widespread epidemics decimating whole populations. As dull and unromantic as it may seem to a contemporary American society constantly in search of unsolved mysteries, the Grasshopper Mogollon and the Mogollon throughout the central Arizona mountains moved away without leaving a forwarding address or a distinct trail.

We feel certain that a few of the Grasshopper Mogollon must have migrated north to join the Hopi somewhere along the trail leading finally to the mesa-top villages that they occupy today. Others may have moved to one of the Zuni towns to be among the first pueblo people to encounter Spaniards in the summer of 1540. And people of the Grasshopper Plateau easily could have moved south to join the communities in the Roosevelt Lake region of the Tonto Basin, although there is little evidence for this. Emil Haury thought that the Tarahumara—native people of the mountains of Chihuahua, Mexico—were good candidates for descendants of the Mogollon. Certainly the Tarahumara represent a mountain agricultural adaptation similar in many ways to the Mogollon, but their genealogical relation to the Mogollon, like that of the Hopi and Zuni, is clouded by the almost total lack of hard evidence. Someday, perhaps, we will know where the Mogollon went.

The Western Apache Arrive

When the Mogollon abandoned the Grasshopper region for the last time, seeking a better life in new country as they had always done, they left the land to its original inhabitants—black bear, coyote, and hawk. The sun beat down on empty rooms, where metates in their mealing bins lay unused, free of women's busy hands. Rain washed in through the hatchways and disintegrating roofs, leaving puddles of water that dried to silt, covering the manos and tools left on the floor. Gradually, the elements took their toll. Roof beams rotted and collapsed, bringing down wall stones and crushing pots, now empty of corn and beans. Wind and rain filled the rooms with debris and mud and dust. No one came back.

The mountains remained silent and empty for a century and a half. In 1540 a Spanish expedition led by Francisco Vásquez de Coronado seeking gold, silver, and the untold riches of Cíbola crossed the Arizona mountains somewhere to the east of Grasshopper. Struggling through the mountains, men and horses alike were hungry and exhausted, perhaps even lost. If there

Apache Crown Dancers at a Sunrise Dance in Cibecue in 1986

were native people in these mountains, they hid themselves well, for the Spanish called it a *tierra despoblado,* or depopulated area.

The mountains would remain an empty land for still more years. Yet sometime not long after Coronado labored through this rugged country, new voices were heard, houses were raised once again, and corn was planted in old fields. The newcomers were the Western Apache, and with their arrival the mountains once again supported the life-style and adaptation that, since time began, had always been the most sustainable and most successful. After the anomalous period during which the Mogollon abandoned their traditional life-style for the one they adopted from the Anasazi, that of village farmers dependent on corn, the Apache reintroduced mobile, mixed hunting-collecting-farming lifeways. And this way of life was just as successful for them as it had been for the Mogollon.

It is oddly fitting that the earliest evidence we have of the Apache in the Grasshopper region comes from Grasshopper Spring Pueblo, where the Anasazi had established a firm foothold in the area. Near the room blocks where the Anasazi had lived, the Apache built round, rock-footed brush shelters or wickiups, called *gowa'* in the Apache language. We exposed one of these structures, and it yielded a fascinating bit of evidence. Wedged into the ring of stones representing the remains of Wickiup 2 was a ponderosa pine stump that produced a pith tree-ring date of 1661, marking the birth of the tree. We interpret this date to mean that Wickiup 2 was built, occupied, and abandoned before the tree grew there, or sometime before 1661.

The Western Apache had come to Grasshopper. A Cibecue Apache man relates a tale of how it happened, so many years past, as told by anthropologist Keith Basso:

> They came to this country long ago, our ancestors did. They hadn't seen it before, they knew nothing about it. Everything was unfamiliar to them.
>
> They were very poor. They had few possessions and surviving was difficult for them. They were looking for a good place to settle, a safe place without enemies. They were searching. They were traveling all over, stopping here and there, noticing everything, looking at the land. They knew nothing about it and didn't know what they would find.
>
> They searched for places that would protect them from enemy people . . . so they made their homes high on the sides of valleys, nestled among the rocks. They also searched for places where they could plant their corn. They looked for these near streams or where there was runoff from rain.
>
> Now they are happy. "This looks like a good place," they are saying to each other. Now they are noticing the plants that live around here. . . . Now they are saying, "This is a good place for hunting. Deer and turkey come here to eat and drink. We can wait for them here, hidden close by." . . . They like what they see about this place. They are excited!
>
> Now their leader is thinking, "This place may help us survive. If we settle in this country, we must be able to speak about this place and remember it clearly and well. We must give it a name."

The Apache had come a long way. The Apache are an Athapaskan people, related by language, culture, and biology to native peoples living in what is today Canada. No wonder they found this land welcoming, green and rich and full of plants and animals. The Apache made the mountain country their land and took from it a good living. The Western Apache, or Apache people occupying what is today Arizona, ranged over a vast stretch of wild mountain territory. They were divided into five subtribal divisions. The White Mountain Apache, easternmost of these subtribes, ranged over a wide area bounded by the Pinaleno Mountains on the south and the White Mountains on the north. The San Carlos Apache lived to the southwest, along both sides of the San Pedro River. The territory of the Cibecue Apache extended north from the Salt River to well above the Mogollon Rim and was bounded on the west by the Mazatzal Mountains, homeland of the Southern Tonto Apache. The Northern Tonto Apache occupied the upper reaches of the Verde River and as far north as today's Flagstaff. Around 1860, before the reservations were established, there were about four thousand people living in these groups.

In 1872 a reservation was created at Fort Apache to be the home of the Cibecue people and the northern bands of the White Mountain Apache. These lands remain theirs today. The Fort Apache Indian Reservation covers almost 1.5 million acres. Cattle, logging, and recreation are the prime industries that provide income and jobs for the people.

The Cibecue Valley is a much better place for farming than the waterless Grasshopper Plateau, and it was probably soon after the Apache arrived in the area that they began to settle in the valley. In the years of conflict between U.S. troops and the Apache, an agency was established in Cibecue and a trading post was built there. Cibecue began to take the place of the old camps on the Salt and Gila Rivers where the Apache had wintered over the cold months and became a permanent settlement. By 1893 there were more than nine hundred people in the Cibecue area, according to Grenville Goodwin. Yet Cibecue was also isolated. Until 1946 there was no road to the main highway—access was by wagon track only. Cibecue remains a "decidedly old-fashioned place where many things continue to be done in an old-fashioned way," Basso writes.

Today Cibecue is the second largest settlement on the reservation. Its people maintain "with full awareness and quiet satisfaction a cultural system and a sense of tribal identity that are distinctively and resiliently their own," according to Basso, and the preferred language is still Western Apache.

Abandonment of the Field School

Like Grasshopper Pueblo some six hundred years earlier, the Grasshopper field school was eventually abandoned. What we have learned from the one we can apply to understanding the other. In both cases resources were becoming scarce, but for the field school it was not a matter of insufficient crop yields and a depletion of wild plant and animal resources. It was a shrinking budget that eventually forced abandonment of the Grasshopper field school. Also, as in earlier times, we tried to make adjustments to scarce resources, adjustments that eventually proved unsuccessful.

The physical plant was the first to fail. Built for a ten-year stay, the field camp became increasingly difficult to maintain. During the 1960s, before we arrived, it is possible that the camp may actually have required little staff time for maintenance, but in subsequent years, duct tape, baling wire, and ever larger hammers were called into regular service to keep critical pieces of camp machinery functioning. The shower drains began to clog increasingly as the wooden floors sagged with age, and swamps developed outside the washhouse. Eventually, as the years went by and the operating budget became leaner, buildings and whole systems had to be redefined, cannibalized, or decommissioned. Unused buildings were scavenged for useable parts to patch vital structures, and many of the buildings that remained were largely held together by the principle we referred to tongue-in-cheek as "molecular familiarity" and little else.

In the end, physical, fiscal, and aesthetic factors compelled us to conduct the last five years of the field school in relative darkness and silence, with no electricity in camp at all. We could not dispense with the small AC generator for pumping water, however, and it remained in service.

Staff was another arena for paring down. During the last decade of the field school, we functioned without camp aides, rotating maintenance tasks among staff-led student crews who bussed tables, washed dishes, and cleaned showers and outhouses. We economized further by having the cook go into town to buy groceries. Those groceries, too, were the focus of economy as we cut back severely on their variety and expense. The memorable 1976 Fourth of July dinner of barbecued steak, baked potatoes, and cherry cream cheese pie devolved to hamburgers and cookies. In the closing years, coffee break gave way to oranges and cookies we packed along with our lunch, which was cold sandwiches eaten in the field. The cook was the last vital staff member to go. Only in 1992, the final year, was there no full-time cook.

We also economized over the years by reducing the number of students from twenty to twelve, shortening the field school from eight to six weeks, and cutting down on the once-legendary field trips. As funding shrank and the camp suffered the onslaught of the years, growing increasingly decrepit and difficult to maintain, a different Grasshopper emerged. It became apparent that we had filled in all the gaps that we needed to fill, had collected all the artifacts that we required, and had answered as many of our pressing questions as we could. It was time to end the field school at Grasshopper Pueblo, to lay shovel and trowel to rest, and to write. We had to make a conscious effort to end, because the research potential of the site and the region were almost literally inexhaustible. But we, alas, were not.

The end was inevitable, and the year was 1992. The year marked a historic moment in time that coincided with the thirtieth and final archaeological field school at Grasshopper. It began as a celebration of the quincentennial anniversary of Columbus's discovery of the Americas. In one of those coincidences that will forever go unexplained, 1992 ended in sadness with the death of Emil Haury, discoverer of the Mogollon and director of University of Arizona Field Schools at Forestdale and Point of Pines, at the age of eighty-eight.

The last field school at Grasshopper was framed by the intersection of an austere budget and untried notions of how to achieve a perfect archaeological summer. The budget permitted only three field staff—Barbara Montgomery, Charles Riggs, and Daniela Triadan—and no cook or kitchen aides. Riggs and Reid cooked a basic breakfast. This team was unlikely to ever have their own television cooking program or, for that matter, to be sensitive to whether camp members enjoyed their breakfast. On pancake mornings, more susceptible diners were reminded that "blueberries do not have legs." Everyone packed their own lunch to take into the field from sandwich fixings laid out after breakfast, and the staff shared dinner duties. That the supper cooks tended to be the women staff members was less for the joy of cooking than from fear that Reid and Riggs might do it. The cooks had passed into legend, indeed.

The desire to have a camp population that would all fit into one Chevrolet Suburban—another penny-pinching move—dictated a maximum crew of seven students. Thus, the director, daughter Erin Reid, the three field staff members, and seven students fitted snugly into one carryall for road trips to Roosevelt Lake, the Tonto cliff dwellings, Canyon de Chelly, Casa Malpais, and Mount Baldy. At Canyon de Chelly we rode horses into the mouth of Canyon del Muerto and enjoyed other activities only possible with a small group. Those road trips are best remembered as family outings, complete with good-natured bickering, friendship, and fun.

The fieldwork, also designed for a small crew, was among the most productive of the thirty research summers. We returned to the ruin of Grasshopper Pueblo, after many seasons at Chodistaas and Grasshopper Spring Pueblos, for the last time to excavate three rooms. Two of these completed excavation of a group of six rooms constructed together in Room Block 1. The third room was selected to provide better evidence for the introduction and use of Gila and Tonto Polychrome pottery.

At the end of the field season, we broke camp for the last time. The final move was not physically painful, because the staff was experienced in the arduous annual task of packing all camp equipment—tools, kitchen utensils and dishes, metal bed frames, mattresses, and so on—to either the old Cibecue jail or all the way to Tucson. The only novel challenge arose in moving the two-person staff cabins, which had served as elite housing. The cabins were modular but heavy and required teamwork and what we fondly call "Chuck arms"—biceps broad enough for a spread-eagle tattoo—to dismantle and move. At the new field school locale in Pinedale, the cabins became student housing, with only the enigmatic graffiti to record their former significance.

The camp buildings that remained—dining room and kitchen, laboratory, three student dormitories, director's cabin, washhouse, tool sheds, gas shed, and two old metal trailers from Haury's field camp at Snaketown dating back to the 1960s—were turned over to Nashley Tessay Sr., who dismantled many of them for useable wood. Unrecognizable now, pieces of the old Grasshopper camp continue life in the outbuildings of Cibecue. The two trailers were moved to the cowboy camp at the bottom of the hill, and the debris was burned or hauled off to the Cibecue dump. All that remains are the stone walkways on a hilltop among the pines.

And so we left. Grasshopper Pueblo returned to its centuries-long slumber, disturbed no more by the intrusions of archaeologists. The Grasshopper we knew is gone. Vanished is much more than a camp that was a short-lived academic community for thirty summers, however. Gone is a whole University of Arizona Field School tradition of archaeological training through total immersion in fieldwork and camp life, of a self-sufficient community isolated in the pine woods of the Arizona mountains. Today's archaeological field schools operate a five-day week near modern towns with their familiar amenities and conveniences but none of the wonderment and mystery of a more primitive time. Vanished too is a rare time of community, of purposeful living toward a common cause, a time of intellectual excitement and the thrill of discovery. The full story of the Grasshopper field school, the last field school in the Arizona backwoods, remains to be told.

We left behind a lifetime's worth of memories. Friends, both Apache and non-Apache, some of whom are no longer with us. Night skies the color of dreams, stippled with the transparent frosting of a billion crystalline stars. Breezes stained with the vanilla scent of ponderosa pine. The spine-tingling sounds of Apache dancers assembling unseen while a full moon rises over Cibecue—mountain spirits whose ancient songs still echo in the night. Watching a daughter grow up under the Arizona sky in a unique place with a unique family.

Today the pueblos of Grasshopper are silent. The Mogollon have vanished. The archaeologists who came to study them have left, and the ring of shovel and trowel on stone is heard no more. We turned to reconstructing the story of the Mogollon of Grasshopper Pueblo, and the tale is told here.

The Apache women who once came to Grasshopper to pick the wild squaw-berries growing near the ruins today buy their groceries at the Cibecue store.

Yet Grasshopper and the other pueblos are remembered. They are important places in the memories of the Western Apache and important in the hearts of the archaeologists who strived and sweated to tell the tale of the past. The past is embedded in the present and is sedimented in the features of the earth. The places have names, and the names tell stories, and the stories are in our hearts. This story of Grasshopper Pueblo has been one such tale, and we have learned as much from the process of remembering as from the product. We offer our story in the hope that others may learn as we did, from twenty years at the place called Nas Tsuggi.

Reflections

Our story of ancient life at Grasshopper Pueblo is, much like our friends the Western Apache believe, a story with a deeper purpose than simple entertainment or a description of what happened to one group of Native American people some seven hundred years ago. We hope to convey some basic truths about the human condition and why archaeology is uniquely suited to discover these truths. What are these lessons of the past that are of value today?

Let us look first at culture—the traditional ideas and ways of doing things that form the collective knowledge of a group of people. Culture consists of information concerning the fundamental realms of ecology, sociology, and ideology that we have discussed here, as well as the socially approved rules for putting this information into practice. We can make a traditional analogy often used by linguists and cultural anthropologists. Culture is abstract, much like the words and grammatical rules of a language, whereas meaningful speech is the actual behavior of putting language to work. No single conversation embodies all the words and rules of a language, nor can any single individual's lifetime of talking be taken as a full representation of a particular language. It is for this reason that a culture, exactly like a language, is the sum total of a people's knowledge.

People often think of culture as being rather fixed and slow to change. Certainly there are pressures within all societies to constrain behavior and to punish those who deviate from specified limits. Much of the transmission of appropriate behavior occurs in the teaching and rearing of children. But try as we may to teach good culture and good grammar, changes do occur, and often they can happen quickly indeed.

Culture, like language, is meant to work for the people who use it, and when the requirements of the job change, then culture and language must change. When these job requirements change rapidly, then changes in culture and language must not lag too far behind. The capacity of people to change the way they do things, and to change quickly, is one important message of the Grasshopper story.

Nowhere is this principle demonstrated more vividly than in the rapid shift of the Mogollon in the Grasshopper region to living in large villages, full-time farming, and dependence on corn. When they first arrived at their new home in the mountains, the inhabitants of Chodistaas Pueblo were hunters-gatherers-gardeners who moved seasonally within a vast territory bounded by the Little Colorado River on the north and the Salt River on the south. Then, as the Great Drought intensified during the 1280s and outsiders began moving into the mountains in larger numbers, the people shifted to year-round living at Chodistaas. Moreover, the potential for conflict between the traditional inhabitants of the mountains and the newcomers was certainly real. The Mogollon people, who had always lived in small villages composed of a handful of households, found a solution when raids and other forms of social unrest threatened to overwhelm their small settlements. They came together, aggregating to form the beginnings of what would soon become the largest community in the region—Grasshopper Pueblo.

The changes that took place in daily life must have been intimidating, for under the circumstances they had created, the Mogollon had to interact each and every day with more people than their parents had encountered in a lifetime. Moreover, some unknown number of these new neighbors were not Mogollon, and, to make matters worse, they probably spoke a different language. To succeed under these conditions demanded that the Mogollon make drastic changes in their traditional ways of doing things, their attitudes, and their reactions. One of the first sets of behaviors to change must have been those related to sociology as we have described it here.

We do not know to what extent, if any, the Anasazi at Grasshopper, who probably hailed from fairly sizable pueblo communities on the Colorado Plateau, transferred to the Mogollon some of the sociological requirements of life in a large pueblo. We know that the importance of the household remained relatively unchanged, that kinship was still the principal means of identification and assignment of responsibilities, and that marriage between ethnic groups continued to extend the network of cooperation and bring outsiders into the community.

There were equally rapid and dramatic changes in the ecology of earning a living. In the span of little more than a generation, the free-ranging, deer-hunting, plant-collecting Mogollon of the Grasshopper Plateau had taken up the digging stick and hoe to become full-time farmers. We believe that this ecological adjustment was accomplished in a short time because of the presence of Anasazi with extensive farming experience living among the Mogollon. It was not necessary for the local Mogollon people to learn farming improvements through trial and error, because they were instructed in the use of new techniques by the master dry farmers of the Colorado Plateau.

The major force for community cooperation and stability was the pervasive ritual component of ideology. The archaeological record, unfortunately, reveals neither the richness of the public ritual nor the subtleties of theology. We are left largely to speculate from the architecture of ritual and the scattered artifacts of its performance. We also infer much about ideology from the mortuary ritual.

The coming together of people from different cultures presented the opportunity for exchange of ritual and belief, for the participation by households in new communal ceremonies, and for the eventual incorporation of these new ceremonies into the ritual calendar of the community. This time of ethnic coresidence was an opportunity to expand and elaborate the rituals that would become the heart of the historical Pueblo religion.

We can also envision a situation in which a ceremonial complex is introduced, evaluated, and ultimately rejected. For example, the platform mound ceremonialism found throughout the Arizona deserts during the late thirteenth and early fourteenth centuries must surely have been known to Grasshopper residents through contacts with platform mound communities in the nearby Tonto Basin. Yet there are none of these mounds on the Grasshopper Plateau and no other evidence of the public rituals associated with them. Ceremonies that employed hallucinogenic drugs or that resulted in intoxication may have been investigated and, if the Hopi are representative, rejected as incompatible with Pueblo theology.

Although the people of Grasshopper devoted considerable energy to evaluating and expanding ritual, we sense, however, that shifts in ritual and, ultimately, in other dimensions of ideology did not closely parallel the extensive changes we perceive in ecology or sociology. It is tempting to speculate that in the mountain communities such as Grasshopper Pueblo we see the emergence of solutions to the problems of new living conditions that may have fostered the character of historical period Pueblo Culture. In other words, perhaps it was the challenges, obstacles, and hardships of life in these multicultural, central mountain communities—and the flexibility required to adapt to these challenges—that forged a new cultural tradition.

Clearly, we have moved far into the realm of speculation in an effort to illustrate some of the properties of human culture. In brief, culture is not a fixed aggregate of ideas but a dynamic, flexible handbook for survival that can change quickly when conditions demand. But the different domains of culture, here distinguished as ecology, sociology, and ideology, do not change at the same rate. This disjunction, one that we cannot measure precisely at Grasshopper, accounts for a portion of the uneasiness and often bewilderment that all peoples experience during times of change. To recognize that drastic culture change can take place rapidly in the relatively simple conditions surrounding Grasshopper Pueblo, when people had far fewer means to cope with change, should give confidence and hope to everyone concerned with adjusting to modern culture change. It is this strength of the human spirit shining through the Grasshopper story that serves to mark the past with a special relevance to the present.

For social and psychological reasons not fully understood, there is a growing tendency in today's postmodern world to glorify the past, especially the Native American past, through creation of myths about the purity and harmony of a life spent close to nature. Of course, this myth, which merely recasts Rousseau's vision of a "noble savage," which grew out of European disenchantment with the corrupting influences of civilization during the age of discovery, is not new. Contemporary myths take full advantage of the European colonization of the Americas during which the biological and cultural horrors throw into even greater contrast the supposed harmony and health that prevailed in prehistory prior to contact. Without diminishing for one moment the catastrophic effects of contact and colonization, we use the Grasshopper story to speak directly to contemporary myths of prehistoric paradise.

. As we have discussed at some length, the people of Grasshopper were extraordinarily unhealthy, and, although apparently in social harmony among themselves, the world beyond the Grasshopper Plateau was a dangerous place. Over half of all the people born at Grasshopper died in childhood, and women during the child-bearing years died at twice the rate of men. Everyone showed severe dental pathologies, from abscesses and cavities to teeth worn to the gum line. Dietary deficiencies and periodic food shortages were chronic, and arthritis was a common ailment of adults. And these infirmities represent only those that leave distinct traces on the human skeleton.

We suspect that the normal Grasshopper adult had a fairly constant toothache, was hungry or had our equivalent of an upset stomach much of the time, was carrying a heavy parasite load, probably had the aches and pains of arthritis, and spent a fair portion of the night afraid of beings and powers imagined and real. We can find nothing beneficial in the physical life of the Grasshopper people for which we would sacrifice modern medicine and contemporary nutrition. Their spiritual life, on the other hand, is to be admired precisely because it overcame these seemingly unbearable physical conditions. In so doing they send a message to all of us today.

When ritual architecture and artifacts are combined with aesthetic expression, especially on painted pottery but also on textiles and tools, we are overwhelmed by the valuable time and immense energy invested in the maintenance and expression of religious life. The people of Grasshopper were able to triumph over chronic aches, pains, hunger, fatigue, and fear to express themselves in uniquely human ways—a dance, a prayer, a bowl skillfully painted, a song or story now lost to the ages. The parable of the Grasshopper story, if indeed archaeology can possess such things, is that the human spirit cannot be suppressed by the physical conditions of existence.

Archaeology in the modern imagination can never be separated from discovery, and even though in North America these discoveries will not be of majestic temples or gold-laden tombs, there will always be in the uncovering of little things a profound sense of learning from the past. Until now we have tried to steer free of promoting archaeology in favor of presenting an objective account of ancient life at Grasshopper Pueblo. By so doing we hope that readers may appreciate what archaeology and archaeologists can do. To us, this is the best possible promotion of archaeology as science, history, and, often, art.

We also hope that our readers have learned what archaeology is not and what it cannot say about the past. Certainly our understanding of human behavior and our techniques for interpreting the past are on firmer ground when reconstructing prehistoric ecology. And although we are developing increasingly more precise ways to reconstruct sociology, we are still a long way from understanding the ideological component of prehistoric life. Given our opinion that ideology was a dominant part of the Pueblo peoples we have studied, it stands to reason that archaeologists have far to go before we will be able to re-create even a small piece of the ritual and aesthetic life of ancient people. Pieces of ideology may be like perishable artifacts of textile and wood that are only preserved under the special conditions found in dry caves and cliff dwellings. But even if we can find fragments of ideology, we will have lost language forever, because in the ancient Southwest it was only spoken, not written, and the spoken word is gone.

It is here that the archaeologists must call upon Native Americans to join in portraying the past, especially by writing themselves about the ideological past in their own words. Because there are many roads to the past, and there are many pasts, the past can have many voices. This book is one voice that we hope will inspire a chorus.

Bibliography

Barnes, Will C.
1988   *Arizona Place Names*. Tucson: University of Arizona Press.
Basso, Keith H.
1970   *The Cibecue Apache*. New York: Holt, Rinehart and Winston.
1996   *Wisdom Sits in Places: Landscape and Language among the Western Apache*. Albuquerque: University of New Mexico Press.
Birkby, Walter H.
1973   *Discontinuous Morphological Traits of the Skull as Population Markers in the Prehistoric Southwest*. Ph.D. dissertation, University of Arizona, Tucson. Ann Arbor: University Microfilms.
Bradfield, Maitland
1971   *The Changing Pattern of Hopi Agriculture*. Occasional Paper no. 30. London: Royal Anthropological Institute of Great Britain and Ireland.
Buskirk, Winfred
1986   *The Western Apache: Living with the Land before 1950*. Norman: University of Oklahoma Press.

Ciolek-Torrello, Richard S.
1978   *A Statistical Analysis of Activity Organization: Grasshopper Pueblo, Arizona.* Ph.D. dissertation, University of Arizona, Tucson. Ann Arbor: University Microfilms.

Cummings, Byron
1940   *Kinishba, a Prehistoric Pueblo of the Great Pueblo Period.* Phoenix: Republic and Gazette Printery.

Ellison, Slim
1968   *Cowboys under the Mogollon Rim.* Tucson: University of Arizona Press.

Ezzo, Joseph A.
1993   *Human Adaptation at Grasshopper Pueblo, Arizona: Social and Ecological Perspectives.* International Monographs in Prehistory, Archaeological Series no. 4. Ann Arbor.

Fewkes, Jesse Walter
1896   *Antiquities of the Upper Verde River and Walnut Creek Valleys, Arizona.* Thirteenth Annual Report of the Bureau of American Ethnology, 1891–1892. Washington, D.C.: Government Printing Office.

Goodwin, Grenville
1942   *The Social Organization of the Western Apache.* Chicago: University of Chicago Press.

Graves, Michael W.
1982   Anomalous Tree-ring Dates and the Sequence of Room Construction at Canyon Creek Ruin, East-Central Arizona. *Kiva* 47: 107–31.
1983   Growth and Aggregation at Canyon Creek Ruin: Implications for Evolutionary Change in East-Central Arizona. *American Antiquity* 48: 290–315.

Haury, Emil W.
1934   *The Canyon Creek Ruin and the Cliff Dwellings of the Sierra Ancha.* Medallion Papers no.14. Gila Pueblo, Globe, Arizona.
1936   *The Mogollon Culture of Southwestern New Mexico.* Medallion Papers no. 20. Gila Pueblo, Globe, Arizona.
1985   *Mogollon Culture in the Forestdale Valley, East-Central Arizona.* Tucson: University of Arizona Press.
1989   *Point of Pines, Arizona: A History of the University of Arizona Archaeological Field School.* Anthropological Papers no. 50. Tucson: University of Arizona Press.

Hinkes, Madeleine J.
1983   *Skeletal Evidence of Stress in Subadults: Trying to Come of Age at Grasshopper Pueblo.* Ph.D. dissertation, University of Arizona, Tucson. Ann Arbor: University Microfilms.

Hough, Walter
1930   Exploration of Ruins in the White Mountain Apache Indian Reservation, Arizona. In *U.S. National Museum Proceedings,* vol.78, no. 2856, pp. 1–21. Washington, D.C.: U.S. National Museum.

Longacre, William A., Sally J. Holbrook, and Michael W. Graves, eds.

1982   *Multidisciplinary Research at Grasshopper Pueblo, Arizona.* Anthropological Papers no. 40. Tucson: University of Arizona Press.

Longacre, William A., and J. Jefferson Reid

1974   The University of Arizona Archaeological Field School at Grasshopper: Eleven Years of Multidisciplinary Research and Teaching. *The Kiva* 40: 3–38.

Lorentzen, Leon H.

1993   From Atlatl to Bow: The Impact of Improved Weapons on Wildlife in the Grasshopper Region. Master's thesis, Department of Anthropology, University of Arizona, Tucson.

Lowell, Julia C.

1995   Illuminating Fire-feature Variability in the Grasshopper Region of Arizona. *Kiva* 60: 351–69.

McKusick, Charmion R.

1982   Avifauna from Grasshopper Pueblo. In *Multidisciplinary Research at Grasshopper Pueblo, Arizona,* ed. W. A. Longacre, S. J. Holbrook, and M. W. Graves. Anthropological Papers no.40. Tucson: University of Arizona Press. 87–96.

Montgomery, Barbara K.

1992   *Understanding the Formation of the Archaeological Record: Ceramic Variability at Chodistaas Pueblo, Arizona.* Ph.D. dissertation, University of Arizona, Tucson. Ann Arbor: University Microfilms.

Olsen, John W.

1990   *Vertebrate Faunal Remains from Grasshopper Pueblo, Arizona.* Anthropological Papers no. 83. Ann Arbor: Museum of Anthropology, University of Michigan.

Olsen, Stanley J., and John W. Olsen

1970   A Preliminary Report on the Fish and Herpetofauna of Grasshopper Ruin. *The Kiva* 36: 40–43.

1974   The Macaws of Grasshopper Ruin. *The Kiva* 40: 67–70.

Price, T. Douglas, Clark M. Johnson, Joseph A. Ezzo, Jonathan Ericson, and James H. Burton

1994   Residential Mobility in the Prehistoric Southwest United States: A Preliminary Study Using Strontium Isotope Analysis. *Journal of Archaeological Science* 21: 315–30.

Reed, Erik K.

1948   The Western Pueblo Archaeological Complex. *El Palacio* 55 (1): 9–15.

1951   Turkeys in Southwestern Archaeology. *El Palacio* 58 (7): 195–205.

Reid, J. Jefferson

1989   A Grasshopper Perspective on the Mogollon of the Arizona Mountains. In *Dynamics of Southwest Prehistory,* ed. L. Cordell and G. Gumerman. Washington, D.C.: Smithsonian Institution Press. 65–97.

Reid, Jefferson, and Stephanie Whittlesey

1997   *The Archaeology of Ancient Arizona.* Tucson: University of Arizona Press.

Riggs, Charles R., Jr.
1994   Dating Construction Events at Grasshopper Pueblo: New Techniques for Architectural Analysis. Master's thesis, Department of Anthropology, University of Arizona, Tucson.
1999   The Architecture of Grasshopper Pueblo: Dynamics of Form, Function, and Use of Space in a Prehistoric Community. Ph.D. dissertation, Department of Anthropology, University of Arizona, Tucson.
Roberts, David
1994   *Once They Moved Like the Wind.* New York: Touchstone.
Smith, Watson, Richard B. Woodbury, and Nathalie F. S. Woodbury
1966   *The Excavation of Hawikuh by Frederick Webb Hodge: Report of the Hendricks-Hodge Expedition.* Contributions from the Museum of the American Indian, Heye Foundation, no. 20. New York: Museum of the American Indian.
Spier, Leslie
1919   *Ruins in the White Mountains, Arizona.* Anthropological Papers no. 18. New York: Museum of Natural History.
Titiev, Mischa
1992   *Old Oraibi: A Study of the Hopi Indians of Third Mesa.* Albuquerque: University of New Mexico Press. Originally published, Cambridge: Harvard University Press, 1944.
Triadan, Daniela
1997   *Ceramic Commodities and Common Containers: Production and Distribution of White Mountain Red Ware in the Grasshopper Region, Arizona.* Anthropological Papers no. 61. Tucson: University of Arizona Press.
Tuggle, H. David
1970   *Prehistoric Community Relationships in East-Central Arizona.* Ph.D. dissertation, University of Arizona, Tucson. Ann Arbor: University Microfilms.
Welch, John R.
1996   *The Archaeological Measures and Social Implications of Agricultural Commitment.* Ph.D. dissertation, University of Arizona, Tucson. Ann Arbor: University Microfilms.
Welch, John R., and Daniela Triadan
1991   The Canyon Creek Turquoise Mine, Arizona. *Kiva* 56: 145–64.
White, Leslie A.
1962   *The Pueblo of Sia, New Mexico.* Bureau of American Ethnology Bulletin no. 184. Washington, D.C.: Smithsonian Institution.
Whittaker, John C.
1984   *Arrowheads and Artisans: Stone Tool Manufacture and Individual Variation at Grasshopper Pueblo.* Ph.D. dissertation, University of Arizona, Tucson. Ann Arbor: University Microfilms.
Whittlesey, Stephanie M.
1978   *Status and Death at Grasshopper Pueblo: Experiments toward an Archaeologi-*

cal Theory of Correlates. Ph.D. dissertation, University of Arizona, Tucson. Ann Arbor: University Microfilms.

Zedeño, María Nieves

1994   *Sourcing Prehistoric Ceramics at Chodistaas Pueblo, Arizona: The Circulation of People and Pots in the Grasshopper Region.* Anthropological Papers no. 58. Tucson: University of Arizona Press.

Figure Credits

Jefferson Reid discusses Grasshopper archaeology with White Mountain Apaches. Photograph by Barbara K. Montgomery; courtesy of the Arizona State Museum, University of Arizona.

Bear Village. Drawing by Charles R. Riggs; adapted from Haury 1985: 150, fig. 3.

Emil Haury dressed for fieldwork in the 1930s. Courtesy of the Arizona State Museum, University of Arizona; neg. no. 56459.

Apache Sunrise Dance at Grasshopper in 1940. Photograph by Byron Cummings.

John Welch directs excavation of Room 13 at Chodistaas Pueblo. Courtesy of the Arizona State Museum, University of Arizona; neg. no. 65411.

Map of Chodistaas Pueblo. Drawing by Charles R. Riggs.

Map of Grasshopper Spring Pueblo. Drawing by Charles R. Riggs.

Men's dormitories at the field school camp in 1964. Photograph by Marion L. Parker; courtesy of the Arizona State Museum, University of Arizona; neg. no. 10476.

Excavation of Plaza 3—Great Kiva at Grasshopper Pueblo. Photograph by James E. Ayres; courtesy of the Arizona State Museum, University of Arizona; neg. no. 12419.

Field school students sort pottery. Photograph by Marion L. Parker; courtesy of the Arizona State Museum, University of Arizona; neg. no. 10477.

Map of Grasshopper Pueblo. Drawing by Charles R. Riggs.

Map of Grasshopper region. Drawing by Charles R. Riggs.

Stephanie Whittlesey uses flotation to recover plant parts and animal bones. Courtesy of the Arizona State Museum, University of Arizona; neg. no. 31545.

Fourmile Polychrome bowls. Photograph by Helga Teiwes; courtesy of the Arizona State Museum, University of Arizona.

Yarn from Canyon Creek Pueblo. Courtesy of the Arizona State Museum, University of Arizona; neg. no. 77524.

Women's string skirts from Canyon Creek Pueblo. Courtesy of the Arizona State Museum, University of Arizona; neg. no. 77502.

Robert Fry and Mark Leone excavate a storage room at Grasshopper Pueblo. Photograph by Marion L. Parker; courtesy of the Arizona State Museum, University of Arizona; neg. no. 10498.

Map of the main pueblo at Grasshopper. Drawing by Charles R. Riggs.

A ceremonial room at Grasshopper Pueblo. Photograph by R. Gwinn Vivian.

Drawing of a warrior from a Mimbres Mogollon bowl. Drawing by Stephanie Whittlesey.

Grasshopper Red Ware pottery from Grasshopper Pueblo. Photograph by Helga Teiwes; courtesy of the Arizona State Museum, University of Arizona.

Cibicue Painted Corrugated and Polychrome pottery from Grasshopper Pueblo. Photograph by Helga Teiwes; courtesy of the Arizona State Museum, University of Arizona.

Canyon Creek Pueblo. Photograph by John R. Welch.

Apache Crown Dancers. Photograph by Jefferson Reid; courtesy of the Arizona State Museum, University of Arizona.

Index

About the Authors

Jefferson Reid and Stephanie Whittlesey are professional archaeologists who specialize in writing about archaeology and prehistory for the general reader. This is their second book about ancient life in prehistoric Arizona. Their first book, *The Archaeology of Ancient Arizona*, also published by the University of Arizona Press, introduces the history of Arizona archaeology and the prehistoric cultures of vanished Arizona, setting the stage for the closer look at the Mogollon people of Grasshopper Pueblo detailed here.

Jefferson Reid is a professor in the Department of Anthropology at the University of Arizona, from which he received his Ph.D. in 1973. He has been director (1979–1992) of the University's Archaeological Field School at Grasshopper on the White Mountain Apache Reservation and editor (1990–1993) of *American Antiquity,* the scholarly journal of anthropological archaeology in the Americas. His thirty seasons of fieldwork range from large prehistoric pueblo ruins of the American Southwest to temple mounds in the Southeast and Mayan pyramids in the Mexican jungle. His research interests include the method, theory, and philosophy of reconstructing past human behavior and culture; the organization of southwestern village farming communities; the Mogollon Culture of the Arizona mountains; and especially the fascinating history of southwestern archaeology.

Stephanie Whittlesey holds a Ph.D. in anthropology from the University of Arizona (1978). She was associated for many years with the Archaeological Field School at Grasshopper. She became immersed in the emerging field of cultural resource management and has since dedicated her career to melding the goals of preserving and reconstructing the past. Along the way she discovered the vital importance for these goals of involving the public in archaeology. Since 1989 she has worked for Statistical Research, Inc., a private cultural resource management consulting firm based in Tucson, where she now serves as senior principal investigator and director of research. Her research interests include ceramics, early farming communities, social organization, and the prehistoric cultures of the central Arizona mountains and deserts.